Peter and the Single Church

Peter and the Single Church

John de Satgé

LONDON
SPCK

First published 1981
SPCK
Holy Trinity Church
Marylebone Road
London NW1 4DU

Printed and bound in Great Britain at
The Camelot Press Ltd, Southampton

ISBN 0 281 03819 8

For Jennifer

Contents

Acknowledgements

The Scripture quotations in this publication are from the Revised Standard Version of the Bible, copyrighted 1946 and 1952 by the Division of Christian Education of the National Council of the Churches of Christ in the USA.

The extracts from *Vatican II: Conciliar and Postconciliar Documents* edited by A. Flannery are reprinted by permission of Dominican Publications, Dublin, and Costello Publishing, New York.

The extract from *Biblical Reflections on Crises Facing the Church* by Raymond E. Brown is reprinted by permission of the publishers, Darton, Longman and Todd Ltd.

Preface

I am not the first Anglican to believe that complete obedience to the Christian gospel must include full communion with the Bishop of Rome, the apostle Peter's successor. Almost from the moment of Anglican independence, a few have recognized Rome's unique authority and have dared to hope for reunion.[1] The pace quickened under the Oxford Movement's emphasis on the Church as a spiritual body. Some followed Newman into individual Roman obedience. Most supported Pusey's account of Catholic essentials with his denial of Rome's particular claims. A few hardy spirits tried to walk the tightrope of Anglican papalism. Their doyen in this century was the Reverend Spencer Jones, whose 400-page *England and the Holy See*[2] grew out of a sermon preached before Lord Halifax in 1900. Rector of a Cotswold village for some forty-five years, he 'inaugurated an important theological dialogue, which brought Catholic and Anglican theologians informally together between the bull *Apostolicae Curae*, 1896, and the Malines conversations of 1921–5.'[3] Perhaps his greatest contribution was over long, dry years to have fed the stream which grew into the Week of Prayer for Christian Unity.

Writing on the eve of the Second Vatican Council, Canon Dudley Symon showed in his *Roman and Uncondemned?*[4] how the Anglo-papalists as a whole had failed to grasp the basic importance of Rome as the see of Peter during the first six centuries. Their successors down to his own time of writing (1959) had, like most Anglo-Catholics, strangely ignored the evidence assembled by T. G. Jalland in the Bampton Lectures for 1942, *The Church and the Papacy*.[5] Perhaps ironically, Symon's own argument ran close to that of the Reformer Bishop Jewel with his claim that the Church of England (at least in its Catholic development) preserved the true proportions of the early

Roman Church more faithfully than did the contemporary papal communion.

My own sharply different view derives partly from starting from an Evangelical base within Anglicanism but even more from the advantage of writing fifteen years after the Second Vatican Council, which has removed so many of the reproaches levelled by Canon Symon. I believe that the time is now ripe for entering into full communion with Rome as she stands. That conviction underlies this book, which therefore gives a highly personal treatment to its subject. Readers wanting a straightforward account of the Roman system as a whole can find it in John L. McKenzie, s.j., *The Roman Catholic Church*;[6] and of the papacy in particular in the very up-to-date *The Papacy in Transition* by Patrick Granfield, o.s.b.[7]

My serious concern with the subject was quickened in the monastery of Chèvetogne during September 1961, where under the chairmanship of Dom Olivier Rousseau I found a method and spirit of ecumenical discussion unusually powerful in breaking deadlocks, a discipline as rigorous in listening as in speaking.[8] Since then so many people have helped to shape my thought in conversation and by letter, not least those who disagree with my conclusions, that it would be invidious to mention names; they will know how grateful I am. Two Roman Catholic friends who saved me from many factual errors in this book are Fr E. J. Yarnold, s.j., and the late H. Martin Gillett, k.c.s.g., whose work for unity was such a practical inspiration. Needless to say, I alone am responsible for the errors which remain.

Ashburton   **John de Satgé**
December 1980

1
Approach

1

The Roman Catholic Church has presented the Churches of the Reformation with a challenge whose force is not yet fully realized. The Second Vatican Council lasted barely three years, but it upset the balance by reopening for discussion fundamental questions that had been closed for four centuries. In doing so it has shaken, if not undermined, the foundations of separate Protestant existence.

The Anglican Communion is notably on the spot. Its separate existence began with the convergence of religious dissatisfaction and the political and other needs of Henry VIII's England. The Settlement that endured was both catholic and reformed, its central claim being to preserve the ancient Catholic faith more faithfully than at Rome, where it was swollen and distorted by new-fangled accretions. Rome herself eventually reformed, but her belated response to criticism became not the Catholic but the Counter-Reformation, so that for the next 400 years the emphasis fell more on the differences than on the shared faith. Meanwhile the Church of England followed the national flag and as in time the Empire crumbled, the Anglican Communion took on an increasingly diversified life of its own. A non-papal form of Catholicism was thus represented in all continents and most cultural groups. In many places it presented itself as a third option between the centralized might of Rome and the thoroughgoing Protestant world.

The Second Vatican Council called the Anglican bluff. Did Anglicans mean business with their claim to be the bridge Church across which the competing sects of Christendom might march to mingle in unity? For at Vatican II the Roman Church declared a concern for unity which did not involve laying all the blame on those who had separated themselves from Rome. A way was found for Rome to deal with Protestant bodies as churches rather than mere collections of individuals. Baptized non-Catholics need no longer feel themselves regarded as lost Catholics caught up in pseudo-churches from whose deceiving structures they required liberation. Willingness on both sides to accept the Christian integrity of the other is the fundamental gain underlying all the other advances towards Christian unity.

It carries with it a great many challenges. Indeed it creates a new situation where all the old differences must be re-examined. Roman doctrine, it is important to note, has not changed. But the manner of proclaiming it has. Two important distinctions have made dialogue with Rome much easier. 'The substance of the ancient doctrine of the deposit of faith is one thing. The way in which it is presented is another,' declared Pope John at the opening of the Second Vatican Council.[1] We shall consider at length the extent of historical conditioning on theological state-ment and the permissible limits of revised expression. That declaration makes it possible to approach a contested matter in terms which are free from long-term polemical associations. The second distinction is the 'hierarchy of doctrines'. This means not that some doctrines are essential and others optional, but that some are primary and others, equally true, exist as their consequences. No longer is the Protestant seeking dialogue with Rome confronted by what seems to him a blandly undifferen-tiated structure of belief.

Discussion which is genuine dialogue between Rome and other Christian bodies has been going on with the blessing of authority for more than a decade. The Anglican–Roman Catholic International Commission (ARCIC) has rapidly produced a body of agreement in the areas of eucharistic doc-trine,[2] of the doctrine of the ministry,[3] and of religious authority;[4] it has pinpointed areas for further common inquiry and it has prevented premature collision. Work at this level is in-evitably confined to the few, but the general atmosphere of Christian brotherhood is spreading. Catholic parishes, for in-stance, have taken over many Anglican, Methodist, and other Protestant hymns. Liturgies in modern English have offended lovers of Latin and of Tudor English but they are creating a community of sound for Christian worship. Scripture readings in English often come from an officially approved Common Bible text. It is to be hoped that complaints in all these matters which are heard across the ecclesiastical frontiers will be met by ecumenically agreed decisions.

Conditions, in short, are more favourable than hitherto to a deeper sense of Christian community which transcends the Protestant–Catholic gulf. Alike in our shared heritage and in the opposition in which we receive from the unbelieving world, we are brethren, increasingly impatient at the need to qualify that noun by the adjective 'separated'. Free from the need to defend our corporate honour, we may scrutinize rigorously beliefs hitherto rejected as well as our reasons for rejecting them. The results can be startling. In *Mary and the Christian Gospel*,[5] for instance, I had intended to explore an approach towards the Catholic doctrines about Mary which would not do violence to the central dynamics of Evangelical religion. I had not thought to do more than find a common standing ground from which Catholic and Protestant could view the problem together. In fact I had unwittingly restated Catholic teaching in a form which left intact my own Evangelical commitments. Encouraged by that, I explored further in *Christ and the Human Prospect*,[6] drawing the conclusion that, unless the Anglican Churches had something distinctive enough to warrant their separate existence, they should deem their work to be done and seek as a priority reunion with Rome. If they still had a contribution to the fullness of the faith which would be lost without them, their priority should be for union with other Protestant bodies.

The present book tries to carry the discussion further by concentrating on the papacy and its claim to provide the earthly centre of Christian unity.

2

The changes in Catholic–Protestant relationships are especially striking in the matter of the pope and his place in Christendom. Indeed there was before very little question about the pope. You either accepted that such a figure was by divine right at the head of the Church, or you saw in the papal system the source and root of all Roman Catholic distortions. The Catholic understanding of Peter's successor was rigidly expressed in the idiom of *Pastor Aeternus*, the decree of 1870 which defined dogmatically his place and his prerogatives. The New Testament passages

about Peter were widely quoted, but it seemed to outsiders that
they were quite torn from their historical setting. Not that that
was as important as it might seem, for many Protestant intellectuals saw little connection between the New Testament accounts
of particular apostles and the manner in which the early Church
actually developed. Less sophisticated Protestants were content
to treat Peter as an example of a certain type of discipleship. To
Catholics, St Peter was the first Pope; Protestants saw no connection between the apostle and the office. Polarization was
complete.

All that is now broken. Ecumenical attitudes on both sides
prefer integration to confrontation and thus attempt to find a
way round deadlock. Vatican II brought into the open
widespread Catholic unease with a rigid interpretation of *Pastor
Aeternus* and set a seal of approval on heart-searchings over the
nature of authority in the Catholic Church which continue still.
Protestant scholars, increasingly collaborating with Catholics,
take more seriously the historical role of particular apostles and
their followers in the primitive Church. An approach to the New
Testament which treats its characters as lay figures for modern
devotion commands little favour today.

A sign of hope for eventual agreement is the widespread use of
a phrase 'Petrine office' or 'Petrine ministry'. Because the New
Testament accounts of the apostles must be taken seriously, the
place of Peter among them cannot be ignored. Perhaps few
scholars today look to the New Testament for a blueprint of the
Church's ministry applicable to all later periods; but many
would agree that 'ministry' within the Church is a service made
up of relationships which will be present in some form or other
in any adequate church organization. Ministry embodies certain
permanent qualities of service. The fact that all the principal
New Testament sources single out Peter among his colleagues,
combined with the persistent sense of the later Church that there
was something special about him, inclines many Christians
today to take seriously a Petrine ministry. The ecumenical
climate makes it impossible to ignore the Roman Catholic claim
that that very ministry is embodied in the pope.

The conviction which underlies my discussion of these well-
worn matters is that the future of the Anglican Churches, if not

4

of all the Churches of the Reformation, lies in returning to full communion with the see of Rome, the see of Peter. The abuses of power and corruptions of doctrine which, rightly or wrongly, led to the break-up of the medieval Western Church have either been put right or have been eliminated by changes of approach. The positive religious truths concerning the way of salvation for which the Reformers stood are now maintained and safeguarded within the Roman obedience. The growing understanding of the papacy as the expression of Petrine ministry to the whole Church makes it possible to consider an Anglican presence within the Roman unity. The principle of legitimate diversity within the Catholic Church gives ground for hoping that such a presence would not only be tolerated but would make its own contribution to the larger whole. The principle of collegiality also emphasized since Vatican II, even though it is far from fully implemented, undercuts many recent Anglican objections to the place of the pope. These matters will be considered at length.

A third principle widely discerned in the Catholicism that has developed from Vatican II is usually called 'subsidiarity'. It is hard to define, being less a theological principle than a practical consequence. The principle of subsidiarity, writes the American theologian Raymond E. Brown, 'suggests that we view the Church from the bottom up, with centralized authority seen as rendering a useful service but not as constituting the core of the Church'.[7]

If the Church is commonly visualized as a pyramid with the pope at the apex and the local churches of the faithful at the base, subsidiarity turns the diagram upside down. The effect of this principle is to distribute authority throughout the Church, from pope to bishops to local congregations, priests, and people: the mother, for instance, teaching her child to pray with the Church acts within the Church's magisterium. In practice this principle recognizes that the Church is constituted by the presence of Christ as promised where two or three are gathered in his name. It implies that decisions should only be handed down from higher authority when they are beyond the proper competence of the people on the spot. Subsidiarity does not conflict with the hierarchical ordering of the Church. It works against concentrations of power which damage the quality of relationships within the people of God, thus protecting the true place of all within the Church's structure. Applying the principle of subsidiarity to the papacy in particular, Brown writes: 'No Catholic wants the Pope to become merely the chairperson of the board; on the other hand, a constant stress on monarchical imagery will do little to unify the churches.'[8]

3

Dr Geoffrey Fisher, then Archbishop of Canterbury, preached a famous sermon before the University of Cambridge on 3 November 1946. His subject was 'A step forward in Church relations',[9] by which he meant full communion between the English Free Churches and the Church of England. He suggested that, to achieve it, the Free Churches should first 'take episcopacy into their system'. Thirty-five years later a like realism suggests that Anglicans should not so much 'take papacy into their systems' as allow themselves to be taken into the papal system.

The ecumenical impetus thus begun by Archbishop Fisher was to prove disappointing. Relations with the Presbyterians, dominated naturally by the established Church of Scotland, foundered on the rocks of historical memory. The Archbishop had foreseen the danger. 'For reasons obvious enough in Church history,' he had said in his sermon, 'they fear what may be made of episcopacy'. How much more acute is this danger when the intention which English people are being asked to accept is the papacy. The fires of religious controversy seldom blaze today, though the problems of Northern Ireland cannot be divorced from religion. Today's Gordon Riots would be over race. Yet the fire smoulders on in the form of distrust and distaste. Racial memories at least partly power the xenophobia which reacts against the primacy of an Italian, or indeed a Polish, super-bishop; while so many Catholics – priests and people – are of Irish, Polish, or other immigrant stock. Reason may suggest that the future will be increasingly international, inter-racial, pluralist, but the emotions, so central to something as deeply held as religious conviction, revolt.

It is not historical memories alone that raise the cry of 'No popery'. The offence caused in many Anglican families by the strict application of discipline in respect of mixed marriages, for example, can hardly be exaggerated. Many who are grateful for the Roman stand against abortion distrust and oppose the ban on contraception, scorning the distinction between natural and artificial methods of birth control. They detect a sinister combination of deprecating sex and ensuring that the Catholic population does not decrease. Catholics are widely believed to be devious, their religious loyalties giving them standards different from those of their neighbours and not necessarily more desirable. Their certainty in matters of faith and morals makes them and their Church seem smug and arrogant. Guy Fawkes Day remains firmly established in national folklore. Its religious significance is indeed forgotten; yet fear of Rome so long explicit in British tradition continues implicit in many current attitudes. Ecumenists who underrate the long effects of history put their cause in peril.

A different lesson is taught by the fate which awaited another result of Archbishop Fisher's Cambridge sermon, the Anglican–Methodist Conversations. There is little doubt that the proposals for unity failed because of widespread suspicion that they represented the triumph of expediency over principle. The particular issue concerned the status of Methodist ministers: was it possible to recognize them as properly ordained, or should they be ordained by a bishop before being recognized? The situation was without precedent, so a new rite was designed to be the vehicle through which God might act in whatever way he deemed fit. The clergy involved were free to interpret the rite as an ordination or not, according to their own convictions; the issue itself was left in the rite formally unresolved – and, of course, all subsequent ordinations would have been at the hands of a bishop. The ambiguity was praised as the agnosticism of faith in face of an unknown situation, or denounced as intolerably disingenuous. The latter view carried the day. The scheme failed.

The lesson with regard to entering the papal system is obvious. It is not enough to turn from the pseudo-democratic wranglings of synodical government with a shrug of the shoulders, saying that if the papacy did not exist it would be necessary to invent it. It is not enough to commend the papacy because it is useful. It is not enough to accept it grudgingly as a price to be paid for the privilege of being fully part of the one Church. The papacy is not an extra, a relic from a more corrupt age still tagged on to the Church but likely soon to be shed or to be atrophied by a thousand qualifications. If the papacy is to be recognized, it must be because its claims are true. There will doubtless be modifications in the exercise of papal ministry, but they will be made in order to remove whatever hinders its true work. The papacy renewed more deeply in the directions indicated by Vatican II will be more, not less, central in the life of the Church.

This book examines the claim that the Petrine ministry is exercised through the papacy. Its structure is simple. Chapters devoted to discovering Peter and discovering the papacy disentangle the apostle and the institution from misunderstanding and myth, using historical methods to pick out the essentials for understanding both. The last section of the book asks whether it is possible to recognize Peter in the papacy. But that question presupposes a good many others concerning the nature of the Christian faith and the role of the Church in the development and preservation of the faith. I have therefore interrupted the logical flow of the argument with a series of studies in the implications behind the Catholic claims. My selection of topics here has been governed by the particular matters which I as a Protestant found to be obstacles in the way of understanding the papacy as Roman Catholics themselves understand it. Experienced swimmers in these waters may well do some judicious skipping here, as indeed elsewhere in the book. But although I have had in mind throughout the reader with no specialist knowledge, my argument is meant to be a serious contribution to the visible unity of all Christian people.

2

Discovering Peter

1

Simon Peter is the most accessible of New Testament figures, so that a straightforward reading of the text produces the material for a biographical article. Even the discrepancies between the four Gospels can be harmonized with only slight ingenuity.

There is, for example, some contradiction between John and the Synoptic Gospels over Peter's origin and first association with Jesus. According to John, he came from Bethsaida[1] and met Jesus through his brother Andrew, on the recommendation of John the Baptist.[2] It was at the first meeting that Jesus told Simon, 'You shall be called Cephas' (Aramaic for Peter which means Rock).[3] The Synoptists tell how Jesus called Simon and his brother while they were fishing on Lake Galilee with the promise that he would make them become fishers of men.[4] Peter's new name was given at some unspecified time – Mark merely mentions it in a formal list of the Twelve[5] and Matthew follows him in this.[6] It does not seem impossible that Simon and his brother had been among the followers of John at the time when Jesus went to him to be baptized in the Jordan, and that they met there. Jesus, the Synoptists make clear, went up to Galilee after John's arrest[7] and it would be natural for the Galilean fishermen to go home at that point. If Andrew and Peter had first met Jesus and had heard the Baptist's testimony towards him, it would account for their readiness to leave their livelihood and follow him.

According to John, Andrew and Peter came from Bethsaida,[8] while Mark implies that he came from Capernaum, where he certainly lived later.[9] Both towns were on the shores of Lake Galilee, Bethsaida at the northern point and Capernaum ten miles south-west. Bethsaida was just inside Gaulinitis, over the border administratively from Galilee. But both towns were in

9

Gentile territory, which would perhaps explain the Grecianized form of Simon's original name Simeon.[10] Either town would account also for Peter's north-country accent[11] and for the fact that even after he had emerged as a religious leader, he had obviously not been educated in a recognized rabbinic school,[12] though equally clearly he was a man of traditional piety.[13] The brothers were sons of one Jonah and evidently partners in a fishing business.[14] They lived at Capernaum with Simon's mother-in-law;[15] but nothing is known of Simon's wife except that later she sometimes accompanied her husband on his apostolic journeys.[16]

It is not possible to distinguish with certainty between an apostle and the general run of active disciples. But when the Gospel writers produced a list of the Twelve, who formed the inner ring, Peter's name always came first. On a few occasions, a select few only of the Twelve were present with Jesus, and that group always included Peter: at the raising of Jairus's daughter,[17] at the Transfiguration,[18] and in the Garden of Gethsemane.[19] Peter was always the spokesman for his colleagues and he took the lead in other ways. He walked on the water[20] and spoke for the Twelve when he declared his readiness to follow Jesus to the end.[21] St Matthew's account of the episode at Caesarea Philippi will be examined later, but he agreed with the other Synoptists that just after Simon had declared the true nature of Jesus, he was rebuked in the sharpest terms for a misunderstanding that could frustrate the Messiah's entire purpose.[22] At the Last Supper Peter was singled out for particular warning and reassurance[23] and his still undiscerning love for Jesus led him to protest at having the Master wash his feet.[24] Afterwards, his boast that he will never leave the Lord is answered by the prediction of his threefold denial.[25] At the arrest of Jesus he cut off the ear of one of the police party[26] but then ran off.[27] He followed at a distance, was admitted to the High Priest's court, was challenged with being a disciple and denied it – and when he realized, broke down in remorse.[28]

Rehabilitation followed swiftly upon repentance. He was favoured with a special appearance of the risen Jesus.[29] St John records an episode where Peter is able to make specific reparation for his threefold denial by a threefold protestation of his love which the Lord accepts, charging him to feed the sheep and predicting his martyrdom.[30]

The Acts of the Apostles leaves no room to doubt Peter's pre-eminence among the apostles. In the shadowy period between the ascension of Jesus and the coming of the Spirit, in the first period of Christian witness in Jerusalem, in the problems of the early community in itself and in its relationship with Jewish authority, in the several stages of missionary expansion, Peter was always to the fore.[31] The climax of Peter's work was reached when the Christian Church was thrown open to Gentiles without the need for circumcision. Since that decision proved to be one of the turning points in human history, it was appropriate for St Luke (or whoever wrote the Acts) to describe it in terms that underline its transcendent character. Dreams, visions, angels, traditional media for divine revelation, were needed to overcome Simeon's devoutly Jewish obedience to the laws which had preserved Israel's identity by keeping the Gentile world at arm's length.[32] But once he was convinced, his conviction carried the whole Church.[33] And although a time would come when he wavered,[34] it was still Peter's acceptance of divine revelation which made possible Paul's mission to the Gentiles.[35]

For St Luke, Peter's decision was also his swan-song. True, he appeared later to confirm his judgement, but he is no longer the central figure. Paul's work had begun. But Luke is at pains to stress that that development was made possible through Peter.[36] Apart from a few references in St Paul's letters and the two letters attributed to Peter himself, the New Testament Scriptures have nothing more to tell us about this apostle.

2

Marshalling the scattered New Testament references to Peter into a coherent whole risks being dangerously naïve. It attributes to the writers the modern ideal of objectively factual reporting and takes no account of particular axes that they may have wished to grind. In any case, Peter is a minor character only, incidental to the main concern of the Evangelists. We do well to heed these warnings and to review our earlier picture in the light of historical criticism. The result may, however, be to heighten the likeness with contrasting details of light and shade.

Documentary criticism was the first in the field and, since it deals with the primary sources to hand, it remains important. The enigmatic John being put aside, parallels between the other three Gospels are so close in places that they must imply a literary connection. Most scholars believe that, where the three agree in all but small detail, Mark is the earliest and the other two have adapted his account to suit their particular concern. One such concern was the growing sentiment that the founding apostles should be seen in a favourable light. The process may be studied in the three records of the incident at Caesarea Philippi.[37] Apart from Matthew's passage about Peter and the rock, the three accounts are basically similar. But Mark's is the fullest, and it is at least plausible to account for Matthew and Luke's changes by the desire to soften the rebuke which Peter received.

The weakness of documentary criticism is that, while it accounts for the literary relationship between the three Gospels, it says little about the period before the documents appeared; and that, on the traditional assumption that Mark embodies posthumously Peter's account of events, leaves a gap of some thirty-five years or more.

That gap was the special concern of the Form Critics, who elaborated a set of techniques to show how material which was preached from the earliest days reached the 'form' in which it was finally written down. Form Criticism isolates each incident in the Gospel record and reviews the circumstances which might have made it important for the primitive Christian community. The advantage of this approach is to explore those vital years before the written Gospels controlled the Christian recollection of Jesus. Its weakness was so to stress the early Christian needs and their place in shaping the traditions about Jesus that no reliance can be placed on the historical accuracy of the written record in which the process ends. St Mark's Gospel, for the Documentary Critic a broadly reliable account of what actually happened (given that it is a selection made according to the writer's priorities), becomes a totally artificial construction where episodes are strung together like beads on a necklace without regard to their original connections, and where any one episode may have been modified by the needs of the Church so that its original form is a matter for conjecture. St Mark in fact tells us a great deal about the Church of his time, but very little about the events which he purports to describe. The historical Jesus recedes even further into the shadows.

And if the quest for the historical Jesus is futile, how much more that of the historical Peter.

The aridities of pure Form Criticism have produced a modified method known by the even more awkward term Redaction Criticism. Interest has returned to the quest of the historical Jesus, seen now in a new perspective. There is no return to the confidence of documentary criticism in recovering a clear-cut picture of Jesus as he actually was. But a close study of how Jesus was presented would indicate the range of lasting impressions which he had made on his followers. Those impressions provide raw material for modern scholars and preachers interpreting the meaning of Jesus for today. Matthew, Mark, Luke, and even John are of primary interest for the distinctive redaction which they made of the traditional material which they had received.

In this light Peter and the other apostolic figures emerge from the darkness of Form Criticism. There is no reason to doubt their historical existence nor, if the impression be strong enough, their personal achievements and characteristics. But those impressions have not been preserved directly from eye-witness accounts, but through a more complex Christian experience. St Paul's references to Peter become newly significant. The existence of parties at Corinth – 'I belong to Paul . . . to Apollos . . . to Cephas . . .'[38] – suggests that, whether they liked it or not, particular pioneer leaders had their own following; and did they like it or not? Paul for one did not. The troubles at Antioch, when 'some came from James'[39] at Jerusalem and persuaded Peter to revert to anti-Gentile discrimination, casts doubt on the extent of the agreement between Paul, Peter, and James which the Acts records. The unity of early Christian teaching, so stressed in the biblical theology of the nineteen-forties and fifties, now seems less striking than its diversity.

Was there a power struggle in the early Church? The received picture is of a single mainstream Christian Church with a shortlived Judaizing right wing, consolidated by the turn of the century into a Catholic Church coherent enough to resist the several onslaughts of heretical teachers during the second century. But is this picture, like that of the Council of Jerusalem in Acts 15, just a little too bland? Did the early Christian movement develop quite so smoothly into the structures and teaching of the Church in the age of the Fathers?

Read with such possibilities in mind, the Acts of the Apostles includes some suspiciously loose ends. There are hints that the followers of John the Baptist remained a force ambiguously related to the church gathered through Peter's preaching.[40] Why were the apostles exempt from the persecution which followed Stephen's death? Does the summary of Peter's preaching overlay an original view of Jesus as God's entirely human Messiah with a later one more in accordance with what had become orthodox standards?[41]

The peculiarities of the Fourth Gospel might be explained by a struggle in the early Church. The last chapter is often believed to be an addition, for chapter 20 provides a conclusion to the whole book. There is no manuscript evidence that the book ever existed apart from chapter 21, and explanations generally turn upon an original writer and a disciple of his editing his book posthumously and anxious to include those fragments of the Master's teaching. But the matter of that chapter suggests another interpretation. It centres on conversations between the risen Jesus and Peter which define Peter's place in the Christian mission over against that of the anonymous 'disciple whom Jesus loved'. In the rest of the Gospel, however, Peter has not cut a distinguished figure. On the resurrection morning, the 'other disciple' outran Peter to the empty tomb, and it was he and not Peter who first believed.[42] It is only in chapter 21, too, that the Lord's threefold charge to Peter reverses Peter's threefold denial of Jesus recorded in chapter 18. Further, it was according to St John not Peter but his brother Andrew who recognized Jesus to be the Messiah;[43] and it was the otherwise obscure Nathanael who voiced the particular connection 'You are the Son of God, the King of Israel' which underlies much of the Fourth Gospel's distinctive teaching.[44]

Taken with the reluctance in some early Christian circles to accept it into the canon, those factors suggest that the Fourth Gospel may be the work of a Christian teacher opposed to Peter's growing place as the leader of the apostles. This teacher is to be identified with the mysterious 'disciple whom Jesus loved'[45] who, as the incidents where he is so described show, was, unlike Peter who misunderstood, particularly close to Jesus in catching the inner spirit of his words. This disciple was probably not the apostle John who, as the Acts made clear, was closely associated with Peter in the Jerusalem church. His identity is unknown. For at some stage the anti-Peter faction which he represented collapsed and his book was taken over by his opponents. It was edited suitably, perhaps by other changes beside the addition of chapter 21 and, under the name of the apostle to whom an apocalypse and three letters were also attributed, admitted to the canon.

That such a reconstruction of the origins of a canonical gospel can even be considered shows how open a subject the study of Christian beginnings has become. Sources of information unknown to previous generations – the scrolls from the Dead Sea and the Gnostic library from Upper Egypt are the best known – have provided rich new food for the historical imagination. The restraint which accepted orthodoxies put upon scholarly and popular reconstructions has gone. In such a heady atmosphere it is good to turn to an enterprise which uses new methods to clarify old orthodoxies and indeed to break the deadlock between Roman Catholic and Protestant interpretations of Peter.

The National Dialogue between Lutherans and Roman Catholics in the United States of America is an ambitious, imaginative project whose findings could be of the widest ecumenical significance. The volume *Peter in the New Testament*[46] is the work of a 'task force' within that project. Its editors insist that it has emerged from a genuinely collective study undertaken jointly by the Lutheran and Catholic scholars who took part.

The book analyses the figure of Peter as he appears in the New Testament. We have seen how greatly such a reconstruction will be coloured by the critical presuppositions of those who make it. An important chapter makes it clear that the book could not have been written much before the early nineteen-seventies, when learned attention concentrated on the purpose of the New Testament writers in shaping the traditions about Jesus as they did. This critical stance is more congenial to Catholics than its form-critical predecessor, for while maintaining flexibility almost to agnosticism over questions of 'what actually happened', it gives high authority to the interpretation of whatever the events may have been which the canonical writers endorsed. The ecumenical advantage of this stance springs from the stress on 'tradition', that which is received and must be passed on. Understanding the Scriptures as a decisive stage in the flow of tradition releases the biblical deposit from that disastrous isolation from the post-New Testament Church which has often relegated Protestant biblical scholarship to the museum. The particular balance of *Peter in the New Testament* owes much to one of its editors, the Catholic scholar Raymond E. Brown.

The strength of this approach, as well as its limitations, may be judged from this statement: 'If the Pauline letters give us an insight (sometimes with a polemical coloring) into the way Peter was viewed by Paul and by certain church factions in the mid-50s, the Book of Acts, gives us a Christian view of Peter some thirty years later.'[47]

The strength lies in taking the scrappy and incidental references to Peter and giving them coherence in a framework of early church life. The New Testament as an historical source labours under the double disadvantage of being a holy book. Since it is a book, it is all too easy to consider it primarily as a literary problem. Many scholars associated with Form Criticism for example wrote about the development of Christian tradition as if eye-witnesses like Peter had not existed. The documentary critics against whom they were reacting had sometimes given the impression that the Gospel writers had spent many hours in the university library at, say, Alexandria, comparing the different versions of a text. But, even when the human factors behind the page have been recognized, the holiness of the subject has erected psychological barriers to realistic treatment. The American study group avoids all those errors.

The weakness comes from the relative nature of the critical presuppositions. Just as the book would have been ecumenically impossible before 1943, when the encyclical *Divino Afflante Spiritu* admitted Catholic scholars to the ecumenical debate, so it could hardly have appeared before the 'new quest of the historical Jesus' had readmitted historical questions to academic respectability. The history of biblical interpretation advances relentlessly, its pace quickened by university expansion and the lust for a higher degree. The last word is never spoken and today's mode is tomorrow's joke. But the American team is to be congratulated on seizing a moment when academic and ecumenical attitudes were alike favourable. Their report exhibits as in a gallery the many faces of Peter as he appears in the New Testament.

The notion round which the exhibition is organized is that of 'trajectory': the developing impression of Peter as it was projected into the continuing life of the Christian community. The impressions form a trajectory because they form a sequence in which the various images of the apostle reinforce, modify, and interpret each other. Thus the first picture of Peter as the fisherman-missionary (Luke 5) merges into that of the shepherd (John 21; 1 Peter 5); and part of his responsibility in guarding the flock is the power of binding and loosing. The good shepherd lays down his life for the sheep and, though hard archaeological evidence cannot rate his martyrdom at Rome higher than very probable, the fact of that martyrdom was burned deep into early Christian belief.

The Greek word from which our 'martyr' comes means basically a witness; the 'martyrdom' sense indicates a witness that lasted through to the death. It may well connect with the theme of Peter as the one who received special revelation. St Paul insists that he was the first witness of the risen Christ and the American scholars tend towards the view that the resurrection played a leading part in shaping the apostolic understanding of Jesus. It may, for instance, have influenced the form of Matthew 16.17–19 where Peter's insight into Jesus is attributed to revelation. The transfiguration, another 'moment' of revelation, is described in language which suggests the risen Christ.[48] The reference to it in 2 Peter 1.16–18 shows how important the transfiguration was in the early Church and how Peter's presence at it supported his authority. In the Acts of the

Apostles, Peter deals with Ananias and Sapphira in a manner which implies special knowledge.[49] His initiative and decision in the matter of Cornelius, so contrary to his deeply conditioned reactions, was made on the basis of a vision[50] and his escape from prison was accomplished through the help of an angel[51] – standard Old Testament indications that revelation was occurring. Two other, related, images present Peter as the confessor of true Christian faith and Peter as the defender of that faith against false teaching. This last function extends to correcting at least the misunderstanding of what his fellow-apostle Paul had taught.[52]

The high reputation which Peter enjoyed as the Church moved into its second or third generation makes it the more impressive that his personal weaknesses have not been smoothed out of the picture. Indeed, the image of Peter the weak and sinful man plays a big part in the total New Testament trajectory. Peter, we may say in Pauline terms, is such by the grace of God alone. He is also Simon and at one level he is Peter in spite of Simon. For if he is a weak, sinful man, he is also a truly repentant sinner. If he once denied Jesus, he has been rehabilitated.

> – a rehabilitation doubtlessly to be connected with the appearance of the risen Christ to him (as hinted in John 21.15–17). The man of little faith has been saved from sinking by Jesus (Matt. 14.28–31); the sinful, unworthy fisherman has been spiritually empowered by Jesus (Luke 5.8–10); and now that he has turned again, he has become a source of strength (Luke 22.32).[53]

Similar trajectories can be traced in the New Testament for Paul, who later becomes *the* apostle; for John, if he is to be identified with the beloved disciple; and for the Twelve as a whole. But that of Peter outdistances them all, even within the New Testament, as the reference to Paul in 2 Peter 3 shows. The American study group concludes:

> But precisely because we have discovered the importance of the trajectory traveled by Peter's image, a trajectory that even in the New Testament is not conterminous with his historical career, it has become clear to us that an investigation of the historical career does

not necessarily settle the question of Peter's importance for the subsequent church.[54]

But it does provide us with a profile of what a 'Petrine ministry'
as a permanent feature in the Church must mean: fisherman-
shepherd-martyr; recipient, confessor, and guardian of
revealed faith; a weak and sinful but repentant man. Peter was
the Rock in spite of and because of Simon. The trajectory continued in the history of the Church, most decisively in the West
where it was institutionalized in the papacy. The interplay
between the New Testament record and later history is complex:
between the historical figure and the trajectory followed by his
image. These matters are open to further scholarly investiga-
tion.

But how does God's providence and his will for the Church
enter into this trajectory? The final question asked by the
American study group is the question of this book. The earlier
phases of the trajectory give a standard by which to assess the
acceptability or otherwise of later developments. As we look at
the papacy today, can we discern beneath the trappings and accretions of history the impression of a disciple's face: that of a
weak and sinful man who is a fisherman and shepherd and
martyr, one who receives and confesses and guards the revealed
truth of God? With that question we take leave of the American
exhibition of Peter's portraits, using some of the insights
learned there to make two or three sketches designed to further
our main theme.

3

Three New Testament passages in particular have been turned
into battlefields over which supporters and opponents of papal
authority have trampled and fought. We visit them now in order
to see what in particular they contribute to the enduring image
of Peter.

Any struggle between the followers of Peter and those of the
disciple whom Jesus loved have been settled long before the
Fourth Gospel was received into the Catholic canon of Scripture. The twenty-first chapter may or may not have originated in
a takeover by the victorious Peter party. As it stands, the

dialogue involving the two apostles serves to define their future roles in the continuing mission from God, preventing, not curing, rivalry among their followers.

The chapter opens with Simon Peter leading his former partners in a return to their previous occupation. The fishing expedition had proved unsuccessful when near dawn Jesus stood on the beach and told them to try once more. This time the net was full. The disciple whom Jesus loved told Peter that it was the Lord and Peter plunged into the shallow water to greet him; the other disciples landed the catch. When they joined Jesus they found a fire ready. He told them to add some of the fish from their catch – the number of fish, one hundred and fifty-three, has been held to symbolize many things – and they had breakfast together.

After the meal, Jesus asked Simon Peter three times the question: 'Do you love me?' Each time he answered Simon's 'Yes' with the command to feed his sheep. He addressed Peter by his human name, Simon, son of John. This fact, together with the threefold repetition, indicated surely the solemn reversal of Peter's threefold denial. Simon is once more the rock-man and as such he is appointed to feed the Lord's sheep. But that task was to be no honoured path of human glory; his death was described in veiled language indicating crucifixion. The commission ended with the command to follow.

It is clear that for this private conversation, the Lord and Simon Peter had moved a little way from the breakfasting group. Peter turned to see the disciple whom Jesus loved following them. 'What about this man?' he asked. The answer was a rebuke: 'If it is my will that he remain until I come, what is that to you? Follow me!' That reply evidently gave rise to an early legend of 'Prester John' although, the evangelist assures the reader, the Lord's actual words gave it no support.

The authorship of the Fourth Gospel, and in particular of this chapter, is of course uncertain and disputed. On the face of it, it seems plain that 'the disciple whom Jesus loved' is responsible for preserving not only the immediate incident – that is specifically stated – but the Gospel as a whole. He is careful to identify himself in 21.30 as the disciple whom Peter had asked at the Last Supper to inquire of Jesus which of them was the traitor.

The inference must surely be that this disciple is the one so close to the Lord not only physically but in spiritual sympathy that it was he who could best interpret the Master's mind. That work of interpretation was not confined to the Last Supper, or to any of the other incidents where the beloved disciple is mentioned. It is preserved for all time in the Fourth Gospel which, more than the other three, draws back the veil from the Lord's inner self.[55] The vocation of the disciple whom Jesus loved was distinct from Simon Peter's. It was no less valid.

Peter's function is more active. He always remained Simon: energetic, impetuous, a leader. But Simon become Peter is no longer the fisherman whose catch must die but the shepherd whose charges must be fed and protected. Shepherding makes a powerful image. Self-sacrificing care is mixed with organizing ability, decision-making, and the management of men. The image is physical as well as spiritual and implies structure, control, adaptability, continuity. It suggests not simply people, but people living in social structures. The sheep are not scattered but gathered into a fold.

Many modern commentators see an ancient rivalry between 'those of Peter' and 'those of John', the Petrine supremacy being challenged. But the chapter as it stands shows Peter and the other disciple together by the lake. The Lord gave his instructions to one and tacitly confirmed the role of the other, in the hearing of them both. Different as they are, both are the disciples of the Lord and they belong together. The beloved disciple, it would seem, is the theologian, Peter the Church leader. Not from Peter would come the profundities of the Fourth Gospel. Yet it was the rough and ready Peter who had to love Jesus by feeding his sheep. Peter's function was practical rather than speculative.

The Church was never a voluntary association of the likeminded, let alone the supporters of an idea. It was a close-knit group of people bound together by a common spiritual rebirth into a distinctive relationship of obedience to God. Their identity had to be protected from the encroachments of the rest of mankind, and to be nourished by healthy Christian teaching. But how might that teaching be recognized? The Fourth Gospel's answer is clear. Believing in Jesus, that he is the

Christ, the Son of God, gives life. Jesus himself is the bread of life; the bread which he gives for the life of the world is his flesh. That giving was an act of love, and in receiving the life, the disciple is drawn into a network of love towards all other disciples where obedience to Christ is no longer that of the slave but that of the friend who enjoys the Lord's confidence. Image passes into image, the unity of the disciples is drawn into the unity of the Father and the Son. Fourth Gospel food is rich indeed. Something plainer is needed as well.

In that context we return to Peter, and to what is often called his 'confession of faith'. The incident at Caesarea Philippi where it occurred included, in St Matthew's version only, the second and the most controversial of the three great Petrine texts:

> And on the way he asked his disciples, 'Who do men say that I am?' And they told him, 'John the Baptist; and others say, Elijah; and others one of the prophets.' And he asked them, 'But who do you say that I am?' Peter answered him, 'You are the Christ.' And he charged them to tell no one about him.[56]

That is Mark's version. St Matthew and St Luke tell the same story, with minor verbal differences. The main change is that Luke has Peter say 'the Christ of God' and Matthew, 'You are the Christ, the Son of the living God'.

The big difference comes with Jesus's response to Peter's answer. All three evangelists agree that Jesus told the disciples to keep quiet about their discovery. Matthew alone adds the commendation which has had such momentous consequences:

> 'Blessed are you, Simon Bar-Jona! For flesh and blood has not revealed this to you, but my Father who is in heaven. And I tell you, you are Peter, and on this rock I will build my church, and the powers of death shall not prevail against it. I will give you the keys of the kingdom of heaven, and whatever you bind on earth shall be bound in heaven, and whatever you loose on earth shall be loosed in heaven.'[57]

In another passage of St Matthew, 18.18, the same power of binding and loosing is vested in the community as a whole when it met formally as the church gathered around its Lord. In John 20.22, the risen Christ bestows similar authority, specifically concerned here with the forgiving of sins, to the disciples who had remained faithful; the power is conveyed by the gift of the Spirit.

The ancients were less worried than we are that only one Gospel carries this passage.[58] Even those in the church of the Fathers who most resented the occasion when the Bishop of Rome claimed the mantle of Peter never challenged its genuineness. Christian antiquity generally ranked Matthew first in importance among the Gospels, for it was the only one with an apostle's name firmly attached (Mark, despite the tradition of Peter's teaching behind it, was little regarded by those who had the fuller Matthew; Luke was not an apostle, though the respected 'follower of the apostles'; once John's name was firmly tagged, the Fourth Gospel came to equal Matthew in importance). And Matthew was, and still is, superbly organized as a vehicle for systematic church teaching. That factor bears on the present passage. The structure of the conversation outside Caesarea Philippi suggest that Jesus was teaching as Jewish rabbis commonly taught their disciples, by asking questions to elicit answers which extended the pupil's own knowledge: integrated into the gospel tradition, it would have the value of a church catechism, which perhaps accounts for its inclusion in three Gospels. It occupies a key place in Matthew's careful arrangement of his material.

The Lord addressed the questions to the disciples as a whole, but although they answered the first question as a group, Peter alone replied to the second. It was correct and all three Gospels agree that, having accepted it, Jesus bound the disciples to secrecy. But first, according to Matthew, he matched Peter's personal reply with his comment to Peter alone. That comment is in three parts: the acceptance of Peter's answer, couched in striking terms; a promise concerning Peter's role in God's purpose; and a second promise relating to one aspect of that role.

The terms of Jesus's acknowledgement suggest that it is misleading to speak of Peter's 'confession'. 'Blessed are you, Simon Bar-Jona! For flesh and blood has not revealed this to you, but my Father who is in heaven.' It was not so much Peter's confession as God's revelation which he was inspired to receive. That distinction makes sense of the perplexing sequel. From that point Jesus began to teach about his coming death and resurrection. Peter's loyalty was at once aroused: 'God forbid, Lord! This shall never happen to you.' Jesus turned on Peter almost savagely. 'Get behind me, Satan! You are a hindrance to me; for you are not on the side of God, but of men.'[59] If the earlier 'confession' had been the result of Peter's own insight, he would hardly have misunderstood so badly, nor been rebuked so roundly. The juxtaposition is striking – and a reminder that any infallibility of a 'Petrine office' in the Church will be strictly limited.

The promise that Peter will be the rock on which the Church is built has occasioned controversy over whether the rock is the man himself or the faith which he has been enabled to declare. The striking parallel between the two statements 'You are the Christ'. . . 'You are Peter' suggests that it is the man himself who is meant. At the same time it is the Peter of the declaration who is the rock, not simply Simon the leader of men, impulsive and unreliable. It is Simon who has become Peter, Simon who has received the revelation. Whenever he acts outside the revelation he ceases to be the rock and becomes a snare. The New Testament has not ironed out the unhappy few occasions when Simon who became Peter reverted to his former self.

The second promise stresses the pragmatic, disciplinary nature of Peter's appointed function. In the house that belongs to Jesus, he is given his master's authority. 'Loosing' and 'binding' could mean making rules and granting exemptions from them, or it could mean condemning and acquitting, and in that case Jesus is extending to Peter the authority which he claimed for himself. 'Both interpretations mean much the same in the end,' declares a recent commentator. 'Peter has authority in the Church to make pronouncements (whether legislative or disciplinary) which will be ratified at the last judgement.'[60] Clearly, however, this awesome responsibility is not to be Peter's personal prerogative. Matthew 18.18 applies the same power of binding and loosing to the whole community gathered solemnly as the Church. John 20.22 gives similar authority, in the specific sense of remitting sins, to the disciples who, after the cross and resurrection, were still waiting faithfully in the upper room; and the power is there derived from the given Spirit. Peter the rock-man is vested with that authority representatively: he speaks for the whole community when it is empowered by the Spirit. Awesome examples of that power in disciplinary action are shown in Peter's fatal confrontations with Ananias and Sapphira,[61] and in Paul's action in the matter of the incestuous Christian at Corinth.[62]

'No one can say "Jesus is Lord" except by the Holy Spirit.'[62] St Peter's historic function was to be the first and the represen-tative recipient of this truth. Matthew shows clearly that Peter's confession was supernatural: however much the true nature of Jesus might be supported from the Old Testament Scriptures, it could not have been deduced from the religious tradition. It was only in looking back to the earthly life of Jesus that his followers understood what had been hidden from them. With Jesus there came on the human scene a phenomenon so new that although the experience of Israel looked forward to him, there was dis-continuity as well.

Peter's function was to be almost in spite of himself the rock upon which the Church's distinctiveness was built; for no one outside the Church would confess that Jesus was the Christ the Son of God. But even so, the Church might have remained simply the messianic fulfilment of Israel, a renewed Judaism, had it not been for Peter's faculty of receiving revelation. If Peter's first 'moment' of revelation was near Caesarea Philippi at the foot of Mount Hermon, his second 'moment' centred on the other Caesarea, the great coastal city and capital of Roman Judaea. It was there that Peter's actions declared the Church to be fully catholic, a community for all mankind which transcended even the barrier between Jew and Gentile.

The Acts of the Apostles presents the centurion Cornelius as a 'Godfearer',[64] which was a recognized religious category in Roman cities that contained a synagogue. The Jews were bound by their religion to keep separate from other men. Their social relations were notably restricted, for, since most butcher's meat had been slaughtered for pagan sacrifice, they could not eat it at a dinner party without, in theory at least, taking part in heathen worship. But though the synagogue was self-contained – church, school, law court, and council chamber alike – it was no ghetto. There were indeed many among the heathen who admired the upright life of the Jews and to some extent followed it. A few only were prepared to undergo the rite of circumcision and become proselyte Jews; but many more accepted a kind of associate status when they lived by the moral law and attended synagogue worship and instruction. They were the 'Godfearers' and from the Jewish standpoint they were the best of the Gentiles, often able to offer valuable influence with the local Roman authorities. They were also to provide the Christian Church with most of its early Gentile converts. The centurion Cornelius was a good example.

The account of Peter's awakening to God's will in the matter of the Gentiles is contained in the long section of the Acts, from 10.1 to 11.18. Cornelius was surprised at his prayers by an angel who told him to send for Simon Peter who was staying at Joppa down the coast. Meanwhile, at Joppa, Peter dreamed that he was told to eat various types of meat which, under Jewish law, were unclean. As a good Jew he protested, but a voice insisted: 'What God has cleansed, you must not call common.' It happened three times and left Peter perplexed.

He was still worried when the centurion's emissaries arrived. However, he accompanied them to Caesarea, taking with him some fellow-Christians. Cornelius greeted him as if he were a god but Peter would have none of it: 'I too am a man.' Evidently his mind had made the connection, for he assured his hosts that God had shown him that he should not call any man common or unclean. Cornelius then told Peter of his own experiences. Peter at once saw that God was at work and that Gentiles as well as Jews were to come into the scope of the gospel. Quite a crowd had gathered, and as Peter was speaking they were visited by charismatic phenomena. The writer of Acts makes it clear that nothing less than a second Pentecost had occurred; no doubt to celebrate the coming of the Spirit upon the Gentiles. The final scene in this act of the drama began when Peter declared: 'Can any one forbid water for baptizing these people who have received the Holy Spirit just as we have?' and they were baptized there and then. At that moment the Church was opened to all mankind; it became the first instalment of the new humanity, potentially as wide as the human race.

The drama's final act showed the decision to be irrevocable. Peter reported back to the apostles and other brethren at Jerusalem, as conservative and suspicious as he had been. He was had up before his peers, but when he told them the circumstances they were silenced. Indeed, they glorified God, saying: 'Then to the Gentiles also God has granted repentance unto life.' And so, says the writer of Acts in effect, it was not Paul, the great apostle to the Gentiles, who actually started the Gentile mission; but Peter, whose own apostolate remained for the most part among his own people. Peter was indeed to waver in his practice at least once – Simon was still alive within him. But nevertheless Peter was still the rock upon whom the worldwide mission as well as the faith of the Church was built and the powers of death could not prevail against it.

Since the Acts of the Apostles describes the fulfilment of the Lord's promise to Peter, it seems strange that St Luke did not include that promise in his Gospel. But he does record another occasion when the Lord spoke to Peter only. St Luke adds it to the forecast of Peter's denial which he shares with the other two Synoptists, varying slightly the order of events between the Last Supper and the arrest of Jesus in Gethsemane.

> 'Simon, Simon, behold, Satan demanded to have you, that he might sift you like wheat, but I have prayed for you that your faith may not fail; and when you have turned again, strengthen your brethren.' And he said to him, 'Lord, I am ready to go with you to prison and to death.' He said, 'I tell you, Peter, the cock will not crow this day, until you three times deny that you know me.'[65]

The force of this, the third great 'Petrine text', comes across more readily in older English which, like the Greek original, uses different pronouns for the second person singular and plural. It should read 'Simon, Simon, Satan has demanded to have you all, that he might sift you like wheat, but I have prayed for thee, that thy faith may not fail; and when thou hast turned again, strengthen thy brethren.' Peter has a solitary responsibility among the apostles, but in carrying it out he may count on the Lord's particular prayer. In terms of St Luke's account of events, this passage lays the foundation for Peter's leadership in the Book of Acts. Its significance for posterity lies in the command to strengthen his colleagues.

4

St Peter held a certain primacy among the apostles. Matthew, Luke, and John all accepted it – the three passages just examined leave no room for doubt. The Acts of the Apostles showed the primacy in action. But what sort of primacy was it? The impression which Peter made on his contemporaries and immediate successors was, as we have seen, expressed in three groups of images: Peter who was fisherman, shepherd, and martyr; Peter the recipient of divine revelation which he lived by, taught, guarded from distortion, and passed on; and Peter who was Simon, a weak and sinful man who through the protection of Christ was yet the rock.

Peter's primacy did not break his solidarity with the Twelve. And it was the Twelve corporately who were to be the foundation of the New Israel. That is presupposed generally in the New Testament, but is made explicit by Matthew and Luke on the occasion of a dispute over who was the greatest among the disciples (we follow the version in Luke). Jesus pointed out that in God's Kingdom, unlike earthly kingdoms, greatness is measured by service. 'I am among you', he reminded them, 'as one who serves. You are those who have continued with me in my trials; as my Father appointed a kingdom for me, so do I appoint for you that you may eat and drink at my table in the kingdom, and sit on thrones judging the twelve tribes of Israel.'[66]

Those words are the immediate prelude to his prayer for Simon. Peter's primacy arises from the distinctive responsibility which he was given. He is one of the patriarchs in the New Israel, along with the others who continue in the trials of Jesus (thus Matthias was chosen to fill the vacancy caused by Judas's defection). Peter's primacy is from within the Twelve and is in no way a matter of lording it over them.

And his primacy did not breach his solidarity with the Twelve. The sequel to his initiative over Cornelius showed that. But it is not easy to be sure how close the Book of Acts is to the events which it describes. The evidence of St Paul, sporadic but vivid, is therefore welcome. The letter to the Galatians is especially valuable in showing how Paul, the outsider among the apostles, won acceptance with those at Jerusalem. He mentions two visits. The first took place three years after his conversion when he spent a fortnight with Cephas but, perhaps curiously, met none of the other disciples except 'James, the Lord's brother'. Fourteen years later he went back, accompanied this time by Barnabas and Titus. He went up 'by revelation' and he set before them the Gospel which he was preaching to the Gentiles. St Paul writes tersely, with an undercurrent of anger. He had evidently been subjected to fierce criticism in the Galatian churches, and he is concerned to scotch it by pointing out that he had long before been cleared of similar charges by the highest possible authorities. On that second visit, he tells the Galatians:

> When they saw that I had been entrusted with the gospel to the un-circumcised, just as Peter had been entrusted with the gospel to the circumcized (for he who worked through Peter for the mission to the circumcized worked through me also for the Gentiles), and when they perceived the grace that was given to me, James and Cephas and John, who were reputed to be pillars, gave to me and Barnabas the right hand of fellowship, that we should go to the Gentiles and they to the circumcized. . . .[67]

On his first visit, Paul had had most dealings with Peter (Cephas), mentioning James almost as an afterthought. Fourteen years later – perhaps A.D. 51 or 52 – he mentions James and Cephas and John in that order, though again he seems to have been concerned mostly with Peter.

There was an unhappy sequel to that second visit. 'But when Cephas came to Antioch I opposed him to the face,' Paul wrote, 'because he stood condemned.' Emissaries from James had caused Peter to abandon the practice of eating with Gentiles. Most of the Jewish Christians followed his example, including even Paul's protégé Barnabas. That last point shows in what high respect Peter must have been held. But the very revelation for which Paul and Peter both stood was at stake. Paul up-braided Peter publicly: 'If you, though a Jew, live like a Gentile and not like a Jew, how can you compel the Gentiles to live like

Jews?' Peter had gone back on his own decision to throw open the gospel to all men without qualification.

The other important evidence which Paul supplies for Peter's place in first-generation Christianity comes from his first letter to Corinth. As in the letter to the Galatians, Paul has to establish his credentials in order to vindicate the authenticity of the gospel he preached; though the distortions which he encountered at Corinth were different from those current in Galatia. In a famous passage he declared the priorities of his preaching:

> For I delivered to you as of first importance what I also received, that Christ died for our sins in accordance with the scriptures, that he was buried, that he was raised on the third day in accordance with the scriptures, and that he appeared to Cephas, then to the twelve. Then he appeared to more than five hundred brethren at one time, most of whom are still alive, though some have fallen asleep. Then he appeared to James, then to all the apostles. Last of all, as to one untimely born, he appeared also to me. . . .[68]

That passage is obviously very early indeed. As in his letter to the Galatians, Paul vindicates his message by showing that it is the original one. He therefore refers to what he himself had received – that is, to the instruction given him by the brethren at Damascus twenty years ealier. That means that it goes back to within three years of the resurrection. Many scholars believe that he is quoting the actual formula in which the basic instruction was summarized, up to the end of the phrase 'then to the twelve'. Certainly the passage is earlier than any of the four Gospels. Its account of the resurrection is therefore the earliest that has survived. That means that within three years of the resurrection Peter was being cited as its first witness. This early formula implies that, however the Book of Acts may re-interpret the events of the first Christian years in the interests of a later theology, the pre-eminence given to Peter in its early chapters is historically justified.

Peter was the central figure in the primitive Church and in a sense he embodied the Church: where he was, there was the Church. He also represented the Lord of the Church, without whom he reverted to being merely Simon. Jesus Christ is the foundation. So are the apostles and prophets, with Jesus Christ himself the cornerstone. But that foundation is visibly embodied in Peter. Peter's primacy does not isolate him from his fellow-founders. It is exercised from within the fellowship.

3

Discovering the Papacy

1

One shelf in my study is devoted to books on what used to be called The Roman Catholic Question. There are modern classics like Bishop Gore on *Roman Catholic Claims*[1] and Don John Chapman's reply;[2] and Dr Salmon's abridged *The Infallibility of the Church*[3] with Dom B. C. Butler's reply.[4] Some are more and some less courteous in their tone, more or less reluctant in their denials. A note of exasperation creeps even into the titles of one or two Anglican books of the nineteen-fifties – *Why I am not a Roman Catholic*[5] and *But I am a Catholic!*[6] Even the most sympathetic Roman Catholic studies indicate by an asterisk those books in their bibliographies which are 'by non-Catholic authors'. There are pamphlet duels such as *Infallible Fallacies*[7] and *The Nightmare of Infallible Fallacies*.[8] In very few books on either side is there any suggestion of today's ecumenical approach. Dom Columba Cary-Elwes does indeed recommend meetings for discussion in *The Sheepfold and the Sheep*,[9] but with all manner of qualifications. He did, however, put forward a number of points where discussion might be useful, which were taken up by Dr Mascall in *The Recovery of Unity*.[10] But before the Second Vatican Council, little if anything was published in English which could compare with the work of such French ecumenists as Père Congar,[11] Père Bouyer[12] and, on the eve of Vatican II, Père Maurice Villain.[13]

Two Anglican works from that period which seems now so remote are especially interesting. *Documents Illustrating Papal Infallibility*,[14] edited and introduced by E. Giles, was published in 1952. The introduction shows the influence of the Conference of Anglican Bishops at Lambeth in 1948, who had reaffirmed that 'there can be no fulfilment of the divine purpose in any scheme of reunion which does not ultimately include the great Latin

Church of the West'. Mr Giles's contribution to that end was to assemble the passages written between A.D. 96 and 454 which were most commonly quoted by controversialists of both sides. He made the quotations long enough to show the original context of key phrases, and indicated briefly the senses in which the principal controversialists had taken them. His sober and modest volume is of permanent value to anyone who wishes to start exploring the original sources.

John Wilkinson's *No Apology*[15] was published in 1962. His aim is much the same as that of Mr Giles, for he notes the differing constructions commonly placed on the same ancient texts. But his method is to analyse the modern arguments.

> I have tried to examine some of the public statements which we make about each other, and to discover how convincing they sound in the ears of those who are being criticized. . . . It is often the case that, in talking about the members of another faith in their absence, we tend to develop a version of their doctrine which is not so much what they believe, as what we disbelieve.[16]

Mr Wilkinson wrote his book after many years of concern for Christian unity. One may suppose that it was in a state of some frustration that he visited three London religious bookshops, two Anglican and one Roman Catholic. He left the Anglican bookshops with a copy of each book on Roman Catholicism that they stocked, and from the Roman Catholic shop he bought a copy of each book that it had on Anglicanism. Many of the thirty-two titles thus collected appear on my own shelves. His analysis of their arguments demands close attention, for it is brief, subtle, and witty. His sub-title was 'a handbook for controversialists'; his chief concern, the quality and use of weapons.

Those two books are valuable in showing how differently the historical texts may be read. For the problem is, of course, that there are so few texts and they are so fragmentary. The answers for which modern investigators search them do not flow naturally from the original questions. Today's questions are generally these: When Jesus said to the disciple Simon, 'You are Peter and on this rock I will build my church', did the 'rock' mean the man or the confession of faith which he had just uttered? Was Peter in a position of special authority among the other disciples? Did he become bishop of Rome? Was there a sense in which the promise made to him could be transferred to his successors – and, if so, was it to his successors as bishop of Rome? Why should Rome, so marginal to the New Testament events, have become the number-one church instead of Jerusalem?

The previous chapter connected some of those questions with the New Testament, which must remain the primary collection of texts. A second set consists of those from the early Christian centuries which refer to the church at Rome, and in so doing show something of the esteem in which Christians of that time hold its bishop. The controversialist's job is to support the papalism or anti-papalism by showing at least its congruence with the early situation. Since the earliest Christians were not chiefly concerned with the question and refer to Rome (when they do) obliquely and in passing, a balance of probability one way or the other is the most that can be expected.

In recent years controversy has changed its emphasis. Two factors over and above a general increase in good will have determined that change: agreed historico-critical methods in approaching the texts; and interconfessional attempts to reach a solution acceptable to both sides. The foundations of the new approach were laid well before the Second Vatican Council, but it was that council, and in particular its Decree on Ecumenism, which made it central to Roman Catholic policy. Many points remain controversial, but they are now to be pursued within a framework of common inquiry.

It was archaeology which immediately heralded the new spirit of common inquiry into the papacy. St Peter's in Rome is, of course, built upon the traditional site of the apostle's martyrdom. Excavations in the years after the Second World War led to a report in 1950 that the apostle's tomb had been found. The Swiss Protestant theologian Oscar Cullmann studied the archaeological evidence together with that from early Christian writings. His conclusion is the more interesting because it was published well before the Second Vatican Council. The excavations, he believed, did not prove or disprove Peter's traditional connection with Rome; that had still to be decided from the indirect evidence of literary witnesses. The excavations did, however, speak in favour of Peter's execution in the Vatican district of Rome. Cullmann's conclusion from the historical evidence as a whole, literary and archaeological, was

> that during the lifetime of Peter he held a pre-eminent position among the disciples; that after Christ's death he presided over the church at Jerusalem in the first years; that he then became leader of the Jewish Christian mission; that in this capacity, at a time which cannot be more closely determined but probably occurred at the end of his life, he came to Rome and there, after a very short work, died a martyr under Nero.[17]

Cullman's statement, cautious, endorsing Peter's leadership in the early Church but with no suggestion that his particular authority might be transferred to a successor, stands at the gateway between the older and the newer approaches. Fully half the book centres on the crucial passage Matthew 16.17–19. Cullman's view of its correct interpretation is worth quoting at length:

> In so far that Peter is the rock, he is such in the temporal sense of laying the foundation as an apostle. In every generation Christ intends to build his Church on the foundation of the apostles, and among them Peter is the most important.
>
> In so far as he is the leader of the Primitive Church in Jerusalem, this also has chiefly temporal significance, and in this respect his bearing for the redemptive history of all later time consists in the fact that he held the leadership of the original Church.[18]

But that is all. There was to be no administrative succession; that indeed is a conception which has no part in the original Christian religion. The first generation, among whom Peter was the chief, was unique in being chosen to bear witness to the life, death, and resurrection of Jesus. On that witness, to which Peter gave essential leadership, 'Christ, who is himself the cornerstone, will keep building his Church as long as there is a Church on earth.'[19] That leadership is not something to be determined by succession in the sense of a link with any one episcopal see.

The mark of the more recent approach is to combine the stress on the historical uniqueness of the apostolic generation with an emphasis on the continuity between the record of that generation and the one that followed it. It owes much to a new interest – to which Cullmann himself has notably contributed[20] – in the theological element of tradition. This changed approach to history marks a scholarly attitude in which for the first time Catholics share the presuppositions of their non-Catholic colleagues. That fact more than any other makes possible a quest for the truth in which Catholic and non-Catholic can share without prejudice to their ecclesiastical loyalties.

2

Those who made up the Church of New Testament times thought that they were living in the beginning of the end. They believed that the Lord would return shortly and that human life as it had been known would stop abruptly, to be replaced by God's public and direct rule through the Lord and his elect. The figure of the Twelve upon their thrones was no mere metaphor. It followed that there was no need to provide for an historical future. No long-term plans are found among the enactments of the early Church and many modern scholars make it an axiom that any trace of forward planning indicates a date after the first generation had started to die off.

We look in vain therefore for anything in our Lord's own life which concerns a successor to Peter. To realize that will undercut tortuous and necessarily inconclusive arguments over whether bishops are the successors of the apostles. The notion of apostolic succession belongs to a period when historical continuity is assumed. The Church of a later day will look back and see as it were *de facto* continuities which in hindsight formed essential links in the providential pattern.

> Now, the Gospel was given to the Apostles for us by the Lord Jesus Christ; and Jesus Christ was sent from God. That is to say, Christ received his commission from God, and the Apostles theirs from Christ. . . . So thereafter, when the Apostles had been given their instructions, and all their doubts had been set at rest by the resurrection of our Lord Jesus Christ from the dead, they set out in the full assurance of the Holy Spirit to proclaim the coming of God's kingdom. And as they went through the territories and townships

preaching, they appointed their first converts – after testing them by the Spirit – to be bishops and deacons for the believers of the future.[21]

That was how it seemed to Christians at Rome about the year A.D. 95.

But rather than search for missing historical links, we should realize that the appointment of leaders in the local congregation was due fundamentally to the nature of the apostolic commission itself. St Matthew ends his Gospel by telling how the risen Lord met the eleven at an appointed site:

> And when they saw him they worshipped him; but some doubted. And Jesus came and said to them, 'All authority in heaven and on earth has been given to me. Go therefore and make disciples of all nations, baptizing them in the name of the Father and of the Son and of the Holy Spirit, teaching them to observe all that I have commanded you; and lo, I am with you always, to the close of the age.'[22]

Since the age has not closed, those conditions still apply.

One of them is the place of Peter among the apostles. The basic problem is not the mechanics of succession, as if Peter was a modern pope whose successor followed him after the prescribed procedure. It is rather to know how the apostolic function was sustained in the life of the Church as it adapted to the needs of historical existence; and within it, the function of Peter. The location of that function at Rome is strictly secondary. The pope is what he is, not because he is a bishop of Rome, but because he fulfils the function of Peter who left Jerusalem, spent a period in Antioch, and arrived in Rome where he was martyred. It is not possible to say why the Peter succession was linked to Rome rather than to (say) Antioch. In the divine providence, it happened that way.

Clement's letter to the Corinthians is probably the earliest and certainly among the most perplexing documents of the subapostolic age. It is in fact anonymous, written 'from the colony of the Church of God at Rome to the colony of the Church of God at Corinth'.[23] But very clear references to it in several writers of the next hundred years or so leave no reason to doubt that Clement wrote it.[24] The evidence suggests that the

Corinthians, still as factious as they had been in St Paul's time, had written to Rome for advice. That fact itself is interesting. The Corinthian church had been founded by Paul. According to one, perhaps the most consistent, tradition, the apostle John was still alive. But the Corinthians wrote to Rome for advice.

Clement's reply stresses the martyrdom of Peter and Paul at Rome (to which it provides the earliest written evidence). It gives specific and general advice, and it claims to speak with the highest authority: 'But if there are any who refuse to heed the declarations He has made through our lips, let them not doubt the gravity of the guilt and peril in which they involve themselves.'[25]

The documents of early church history are in the nature of the case fragmentary. The reader working through the selection of texts most used by controversialists for or against the papacy will find it hard not to be impressed by the natural way in which local churches in doubt at some point appealed to Rome, and the Romans found it natural to respond. The Peter function seemed to be located there.

Political reasons are often suggested. Christianity spread within the limits of the Roman world, its journeys made possible by the *pax Romana*. What more natural development than to locate at Rome any central authority which the new movement might need? Its authority would be supported by the prestige of the imperial capital. But this explanation ignores the Empire's hostility to the Christians which provoked some of them to equate Rome with Babylon and see there at least a type of the Anti-Christ itself. It also supposes a unified strategic approach which accords ill with the surviving records.

Dr Henry Chadwick discussed the problem in his inaugural lecture at Oxford in 1959, *The Circle and the Ellipse*. 'Primitive Christianity is a circle with Jerusalem at its centre,' he wrote. 'The first Christians were divided from their fellow-countrymen only by the fact that they believed the long expectations of God's people had indeed been fulfilled: Jesus of Nazareth was God's Anointed.'[26] The failure of most Jews to respond and the opening of the faith to Gentiles posed great problems. Hence the importance of Paul's recognition by the 'pillars' at Jerusalem: for his work to prosper, the original leaders must recognize Gentile converts, in Dr Chadwick's phrase, 'as true and full members, albeit extra-mural members, of the one Church of God'.[27] The one condition which the Jerusalem apostles laid down was that Gentile Christians should support the Jerusalem church by sending money, as the synagogues of the Jewish dispersion supported the Temple at Jerusalem. 'The entire story', Dr Chadwick concludes, 'has a single theological presupposition as its foundation: Christendom has a geographical centre and this is Jerusalem. Gentile Christians might be free from Judaism; they remained debtors to Zion.'[28]

The Jerusalem church had a chequered career. James the Lord's brother, who, as we saw, was the first to be named among those who met Paul at his second visit, remained in charge until he was murdered about A.D. 65.[29] Something not unlike the Islamic caliphate seems to have developed, for 'those apostles and disciples of the Lord who were still surviving met together from all quarters and, together with our Lord's relatives after the flesh . . . took counsel, all in common . . .' to elect a successor to James. Symeon, son of Clopas, was 'approved worthy of the throne of the community in that place'. He was reputed to be the Lord's cousin, Clopas being Joseph's brother.[30] All this happened on the eve of the Jewish revolt of A.D. 66 (the nationalist defeat was rumoured to be a punishment for James's murder). The Christians, however, were not involved in the actual fall of Jerusalem, for they had been warned by revelation and had removed themselves to Pella in Peroea.[31]

Symeon or Simon is said to have presided over the church at Jerusalem for many years, so the Christian community must have returned to the city. He was martyred in the reign of Trajan (98–117), it was said at the age of 120. Interestingly, he was denounced to the authorities by certain 'heretics' as a member of the royal house of David, and as such presumably suspect as a potential focus for nationalist revolt.[32] Symeon's death ended the leadership of Jesus's family at Jerusalem, for the shadowy figures who followed him in rapid succession, though of the circumcision, were not of 'the family'.[33] The revolt against the Romans under Bar Cochba (132) ended the succession of Jewish bishops. The bishops of the Roman city of Aelia Capitolina which Hadrian built on the ruins of Jerusalem were, like all its other permitted citizens, Gentiles.[34]

Eusebius, the early church historian whom we have been following, preserves also the memory of another branch of the Lord's earthly family, the grandsons of Jude, 'his brother after the flesh, as he was called'. These men were denounced as members of the royal house of David during the reign of Domitian, but since they were humble folk devoid of all political pretension, they were set free. When they were released, 'they ruled the churches, inasmuch as they were both martyrs and of the Lord's family; and, when peace was established, remained alive until the time of Trajan'. The author whom Eusebius was quoting, Hegesippus, saw no contradiction between their rule and that of their kinsman Symeon.[35]

The mystique of Jerusalem long outlasted the end of the Jewish church there; and the Gentile church that followed it felt itself the guardian of holy traditions. Even before the legalizing of the Church under Constantine opened up a veritable tourist trade, Christians from far afield had been concerned with the Holy Places. On a theological, or mythological, level, the belief that the Lord would return to reign with the saints for a thousand years in a renewed Jerusalem ('Chiliasm' or 'Millenarianism') was shared to some degree by many of the great Fathers of the third and fourth centuries, and similar notions of cataclysmic events centring on Jerusalem are to this day not wholly absent from the Christian mind.

The story of the Rome idea, as Dr Chadwick calls it,[36] ran parallel to the Jerusalem idea, though it developed later. In the West it was natural, for St Paul had written to Rome alone of the Western churches and no other Western city could claim apostolic foundation, let alone the martyrdom of two apostles. The second century saw a rift between Rome and the East over the proper date for celebrating Easter. Around A.D. 125 Bishop Polycarp of Smyrna came to discuss the matter with the bishop of Rome, Anicetus. Both could cite venerable precedent for their custom, and they agreed to differ without breach of fellowship. Half a century later, however, Bishop Victor of Rome excommunicated Polycrates, the leader of the Asian bishops who kept their ancient tradition. Such high-handedness was more than the great theologian Irenaeus, an Easterner himself who had become bishop of Lyons, could stand: 'A man well-named, for he was a peacemaker both in name and in character,' commented Eusebius. Irenaeus urged Victor to continue his predecessor's policy of agreeing to differ.[37]

'Victor's actions disclosed to the Greek East that Rome is thinking of Christendom as a circle centred upon itself,' wrote Dr Chadwick.[38] Other incidents occurred in the next century which led the Easterners to remind the Romans that the apostles Peter and Paul had come from the East, even though they were martyred in Rome. But Roman prestige grew, and churches quarrelling among themselves sometimes appealed to Rome as arbiter. By the fourth century the bishop of Rome was generally accepted as patriarch of the West. 'And if it is to be asked wherein lies the superiority of Rome to Antioch, of which Peter had also been bishop,' Dr Chadwick remarks, 'the answer comes that Rome's unique distinction lies in the possession of the remains of the martyred apostles. Rome had got the bones.'[39] There was really no way round that. Awareness of Jerusalem's earlier primacy indeed survived, to be revived notably by bishops in Gaul or Britain who wished to counter the Roman claims; but those claims in the event proved more powerful. And with the decline of secular Rome, a whole new range of factors came into play.

Dr Chadwick found the seeds of this development in the New Testament itself, particularly in the missionary attitudes of St Paul. Faced with the general Jewish rejection of the Messiah, Paul turned to the Gentiles, his mission to them being complementary to that of Peter and John to the Jews. He wrestled with the theoretical problems in his letter to the Romans, chapters 9 to 11. The Jews had been temporarily blinded, but the light that had passed to the Gentiles was to provoke the Jews to jealousy and so restore them to their proper place in the divine scheme. In the end, all Israel will be saved, together with the fullness of the Gentiles. The Gentiles are like a wild branch grafted into a vine; if it is not fruitful, it will be cut off. 'Gentile Christianity', declares Dr Chadwick, 'is a parenthetic, Protestant movement to recall Catholic Judaism to its true vocation.'[40]

In the event the balance between the two parts of the

Church tilted overwhelmingly the other way. With the growing gulf between Christian and Jew, Jerusalem as a focus became increasingly spiritualized. When eventually the Roman Empire adopted Christianity, 'Roman' and 'Christian' became almost interchangeable terms. No longer could the two beasts in St Matthew's account of the entry into Jerusalem be expounded to 'symbolize the two Churches, Jewish and Gentile, who in double harness draw the chariot of the Lord's triumph'.[41] At first the problem had been how a Gentile could be a Christian; by the fourth century, it was how a Jew could be one.

St Paul had modified the original conception of the Church as a circle of Christian Jews centring round the apostles at Jerusalem so that it became an ellipse whose second focus is the Church of the Gentiles. The thrust of Paul's missionary effort led him to face all manner of dangers in order to reach Rome. There he taught and there he died, and there died also his great fellow-apostle to the Jews, Peter. That combination of circumstances meant the eventual eclipse of Jerusalem. Dr Chadwick ends by pointing the contrast between the splendour of St Peter's at Rome and the isolation and neglect of St Paul outside the Walls. 'There is perhaps irony here,' he reflects. 'For if there is one man who more than any other one man may be regarded by the historian as the founder of the papacy, that man is surely St Paul.'[42]

3

It is easier to say why Jerusalem ceased to be the mother of all the Churches than to explain how Rome came to wear that mantle. It is not even known what brought St Peter to Rome. The cautious language of a modern Catholic scholar emphasizes the uncertainty. 'Peter's going to Rome must be ascribed to the impulse of the Spirit pervading the Church as well as to Peter's own decision. And it is not impossible that the link between Rome and the succession to Peter was based on a decision of the Church towards the end of the apostolic age.'[43]

Equally obscure is the process by which Peter's traditional office was established in a structure that may be identified throughout all later history. But in that the primacy of the

Roman bishop is no different from any other major church institution. Later generations understood that the apostles had
appointed bishops to be pastors in each local church, assisted by
presbyters and deacons. The few records that have survived
suggest a less tidy process, with considerable difference between
one local church and another; but then, even the list of books
that made up the canonical New Testament was not agreed for
some time. But by the middle of the third century all Christian
churches were organized locally into groups presided over by a
single bishop and each church recognized the others by the
common teaching of which the bishop was the source and guardian. The New Testament shows that the earliest Christian
groups were variously organized in ways that might have given
rise to something more like presbyterian or independent than
episcopal systems. But in fact they did not, and until the
medieval unity exploded at the Reformation, no surviving
Christian group seems to have questioned the rightness of
episcopacy.

'Life arose in the primordial broth by the action of sunlight
on simple molecules.'[44] The analogy of primeval broth
illuminates ecclesiastical as well as biochemical origins. It is of
course as old as the Book of Genesis. The picture is of a boiling
cauldron in which many shapes definable from later experience
swirl around, tangling and twining with each other as the broth
bubbles and heaves. Later, when it has cooled, the ingredients
will have formed a pattern and the relationship between them
will be more stable. Thus the element of pastoral oversight, the
bishop's particular service, had previously been exercised in
other ways. Just as the broth is not original but results from the
interaction of many ingredients, so existing experience gave
substance to early church life. The constitution of the Jewish
synagogue and the qualities required in officials of the Roman
Empire were among the molecules. The sunlight which acted
upon them was the Holy Spirit; or, if you prefer not to dignify
the result with such high authority, the hard experience of
history which made sure that only the fittest form of government
was allowed to survive.

There is, of course, the view that the early catholicism which
suppressed all other forms of Christian life was a sad mistake.

We shall consider that view later, but it is no help in the immediate task of discovering the papacy.

> The Roman papacy passed from a rudimentary to a fully developed stage. Under the stress of circumstances, in the course of history, many alien tasks accrued to the popes, including the government of the Papal States. Then, as political and social conditions changed, the popes freed themselves once more from such tasks, though often only slowly, hesitantly, and unwillingly, fearing that the loss of worldly power might involve restrictions on their spiritual mission.[45]

The scholar previously quoted, Georg Schwaiger, summarizes in that fashion nearly 2000 years of history. And in so doing he calls attention to the chief difficulty facing anyone who attempts to discover the papacy with some understanding: The institution is at once political and spiritual, but which is it at heart? Will its inmost secrets open to a theological key, or should we pick the lock with sociology?

The papacy poses in acute form the problem in appreciating all church institutions, for the Church is a fact at once theological and sociological. That point needs especial emphasis at a time when the Church as an institution stands low in general esteem. The terms 'Church' and 'Christianity' are now used as if they were interchangeable but the formalism of the Church is often contrasted unfavourably with the vitality of Christianity. That can only happen in a situation where the Church has influenced public opinion long enough for some of its sentiments to have rubbed off on to the norms of everyday life. The ancient world in which the Church was new could hardly have isolated Christianity from the institution that promoted it. Indeed the notion of Christianity is in the early centuries an anachronism. In the Roman world, the Christians were not those who professed liberal sentiments of general good will. They were members of a closed and secret corporation widely regarded as subversive, liable to be punished as enemies of gods and men. Christianity was not a philosophy which an individual might choose to live by, an alternative to stoicism or epicureanism. It was an institution, a life, a new age into which its members had to be reborn.

It is not therefore possible to separate the teaching from the institution like wheat from chaff. The teaching cannot exist apart from the organization and the organization is part of the teaching. Its truth cannot be abstracted from history. Yet history changes and truth does not. Though the truth cannot be taken out of its historical vehicle, it cannot be wholly confined within it. The vehicle itself will change, and at any given time it will contain disposable as well as essential elements. The theologian who tries to distinguish between them must use the evidence of historian and sociologist also.

A history of the papacy can hardly be written in a single book, let alone a short chapter. Yet some skeleton of historical development is necessary for understanding an institution which has shown itself able to adapt so well to changing events. Its first distinct period ran from the beginning until early in the fourth century the Roman Empire recognized the Church's right to exist. At this time the role of the papacy was by later standards rudimentary. Rome, the church of two martyred apostles, the founders of the mission both to Jews and Gentiles, was appealed to in certain situations. It was a resource somehow superior to that provided by other local churches. But the ecclesiastical broth was still swirling too hard for the permanent forms to be clearly seen.

Already certain features had appeared, however, which made clear the solution of one perennial problem. The Church was defined in the groups of people in a particular place who met around their bishop. But though the churches were thus many, they were also one. The bishop represented Christ who was believed to be present in the local gathering. And Christ was not many but one. There was thus a hidden ('mystical') unity which meant that members of geographically separated churches belonged to the one Church: The one Church was localized in the many churches. The bishop around whom the local church gathered was also the representative of the universal episcopate. Evidently this spiritual fact required organizational expression. Once more the churches looked to the civil power for guidance. Bishops of the churches in those towns which had administrative responsibilities over other towns in the region took on additional responsibilities for the churches in the smaller towns.

45

Councils of bishops from churches in the same secular unit of administration met to consider matters of common concern. The process was complicated, and unfortunately the modern terms originally meant something different; but, to put it briefly in modern terms, the churches round the bishops each in his diocese formed part of a larger structure of provinces where certain bishops held also responsibilities as metropolitans or primates.

Imperial recognition of the Church was a piece of realism, for the Church was already a force in the Empire. A new capital, Constantinople, meant that the bishop of that city joined his colleagues in the ancient sees of Jerusalem, Antioch, and Alexandria in a category of particular eminence soon to be known as patriarchates. As for the bishop of Rome, the former imperial capital where the church was that of the martyred apostles Peter and Paul was endowed with a new authority: secular in one sense, yet, since Caesar had now acknowledged Christ, sacred as well. The popes (that title, meaning father, was not originally reserved for the bishop of Rome) of the fourth and fifth centuries played relatively minor parts in the intense theological life of the time, though their arbitration was sometimes sought. In the mid-fifth century, however, Pope Leo's intervention could evoke the cry, 'Peter has spoken through Leo!'

A century or so later, Pope Gregory the Great occupied a position where secular authority was almost as great as spiritual. The Roman Empire was in its last phase. There was no emperor in the West, the final holder of that office having yielded authority to his colleague at Constantinople (Augustus's empire had been divided administratively for 200 years). The mantle of Caesar in the West had fallen on the successors of Peter. So it was that around A.D. 725 the Northumbrian monk Bede found it natural to put the pope's authority alongside that of the emperor:

> In the year of our Lord 582 Maurice, 54th successor to Augustus, became Emperor, and ruled for 21 years. In the tenth year of his reign Gregory, an eminent scholar and administrator, was elected Pontiff of the apostolic Roman see, and ruled it for thirteen years six months and ten days.[46]

46

That same Gregory could write 'To our excellent son, the most glorious King Ethelbert, King of the English, the Bishop Gregory'.[47]

The pope's twin roles of spiritual father and guardian of Roman values lie at the root of the papacy. If any one date is specially important, it must be A.D. 321, when Constantine issued an edict allowing the Church as such to hold property. The faithful were then able to show their zeal by giving money and land. The Roman church, which preserved the martyred remains as well as the faith of Peter and Paul, attracted many gifts. The 'patrimony of Peter', as it was called, increased greatly throughout the 500s until by the time of Gregory it included large areas of land widely scattered round the Mediterranean as well as huge tracts in Italy itself. The papacy thus became a temporal power on a scale which made relations with the emperor at Constantinople difficult. The pope himself was a major power in the fluid political scene of what was becoming Western Europe. In the eighth century Pepin king of the Franks made two outstanding donations in return for Pope Stephen II's support against the Lombards; and on Christmas Day 800 Pope Leo III crowned Pepin's son Charlemagne Holy Roman Emperor. The medieval scenario was now prepared with the pope in his dual role of father of the Church throughout the Western world and a political power in his own right within that world.

One legacy was, of course, a constant struggle with the secular rulers and hereditary dukedoms or kingdoms which they established. Appointment of bishops was particularly contentious, for not only were many sees possessed of great wealth, but bishops who owed their appointment to Rome would be foreign agents in the king's domain; with the papal state a power in its own right, all manner of diplomatic considerations were involved. The papal power was indeed sustained by moral and religious sanctions, but unfortunately its legal claims were later buttressed by certain documents that were undoubtedly forged.

But even politically the pope did not need such dubious support. The collapse of imperial authority in the West deprived the lands to the west of the Adriatic and the Alps of any cohesive centre. The Church, its diocesan structure modelled on Roman administrative divisions, was the obvious successor. The very title Roman Pontiff showed how fully the bishop of Rome had filled the vacant imperial function. The alliance between the popes and the Carolingian Franks ensured a bridge across which the ancient values passed to civilize and christianize the new nations; papal support for the Benedictine monks made for stability in the most turbulent times. Dark and dangerous years indeed followed when the spiritual fire burned low, the Church being almost overwhelmed by the need to preserve its lands; but never entirely.

The high Middle Ages saw a titanic struggle between Church and Empire as popes and Western emperors vied for supremacy. A smaller version of the struggle became a principal theme in English history after the Norman Conquest. Henry VIII's insistence on supremacy which triggered off the Reformation was but the last of a long line of such assertions, and the papal Bull excommunicating Elizabeth I and freeing her subjects from their sworn allegiance was, from the medieval point of view, a standard move. But of course the Middle Ages had passed and with them went also the notion of Christendom as a political and religious reality lying behind the several nations.

The Reformation in one aspect was a protest against the extent to which the political aspects of papacy had overridden its spiritual responsibilities. The nations in their new autonomy decided for or against the old religion. But Catholic as well as Protestant sovereigns were monarchs to a degree of absoluteness which tolerated no interference from a spiritual father who was also a rival sovereign. The theoretical issues involved will be discussed in a later chapter. The Church meanwhile was well served by Catholic reformers who ended many of the abuses which had so weakened Rome's spiritual credibility in the later Middle Ages. But it was not until the Enlightenment with its rationalism and its hatred of priestcraft had deprived the papacy of all its lands except the Vatican itself that the Church was free enough from worldly concerns to be in practice what in theory it always was.

4

The papacy is still a sovereign state. Sociologically, the declaration of the First Vatican Council of the pope's infallibility may read as compensation for the loss of temporal power inflicted during the unification of Italy. But the Vatican State's survival through the frenzy of Europe's twentieth-century self-destruction, achieved largely through Pius XI's Concordat with Mussolini, suggests that the aspect of papacy which started when the faithful were allowed to honour the shrine of the martyred apostles, may be more vital than might be supposed. The visitor to Rome is well aware of it, though recent popes have simplified much of the ceremonial. Unfortunately, however, it is seldom considered in theological approaches to the Roman enigma.

A convenient description of the modern Vatican State is given by Conrado Pallenberg in his *Vatican Finances*.[48] 'As a whole,' writes Signor Pallenberg, an Italian lawyer and journalist who has been Rome correspondent of *The Sunday Telegraph,* 'the smallest state in the world could be described as a vast office and self-sufficient hotel run quietly, efficiently, and economically on a non-profit basis by an assorted crowd of guards, policemen, courtiers, ushers, clerks, manual labourers, priests, monks, friars, and nuns.'[49]

He makes the point that the pope, an absolute monarch responsible only to God and his own conscience, is not considered infallible when he exercises his temporal and administrative powers.

The pope governs through the Curia. The word means 'court', but that has to be understood in a special sense. Immediately below him come the cardinals, holders of an ancient office which has changed much across the centuries. The rank of cardinal is not, of course, a holy order in the sense of bishop, priest, or deacon, but an honorary and administrative office. The pope appoints the cardinals to their college; they really come into their own when after the death of the pope they elect his successor. Members of the college divide broadly into those cardinals who hold a see in their own country and those who are based in Rome where they have permanent administrative responsibilities. A synod of bishops has recently been created, its members drawn from the Episcopal Conference of each country, but its terms of reference are limited and its decisions lack mandatory force. Another recent development is the appointment of a Secretary of State to be the chief executive of the papacy. The Secretary of State 'combines the functions of Prime Minister, Home Minister, and Foreign Minister'[50] in that all important threads pass through his hands. His secretariat is the core of the Curia. The inquiries of Peter Hebblethwaite have shown the enormous power which administrative reform put in the hands of a recent 'Sostituto,' as the official who controls the day-to-day running of the Secretariat of State is entitled. 'The effect of restructuring the Curia was to make the Sostituto the hour-glass linking Pope and Church.'[51]

The Curia falls into three principal divisions. There are the various services involved in the pope's temporal and administrative power: economic affairs, administration of revenues, Institute for Religious Works, the Governor of the Vatican City who is responsible for the upkeep of all its services – museums, library, radio, observatory, and the summer villa at Castel Gandolfo. The second main division includes the extensive diplomatic service. The third division is the one which theologians mostly mean when they speak about the Curia, the bodies in Rome who are 'head office' for many Catholic interests. Through them the pope exercises his spiritual, doctrinal, and juridical control. Most of them are Congregations, departments normally presided over by a cardinal: for Bishops, for the Oriental Churches, for Discipline of the Sacraments, for Liturgy, for Religious Orders. The most important in many ways is the Sacred Congregation for the Doctrine of the Faith, formerly known as the Holy Office. There are also Secretariats, such as that for the Promotion of the Unity of Christians.

The Roman Curia remains 'the most unknown and impenetrable level of Roman life',[52] yet its decisions touch the lives of Catholics at countless points. Its basic attitudes were formed by the First Vatican Council which ended hastily but never closed formally when the Franco–Prussian War caused the withdrawal of its French military protectors. The curial mentality in the decades that followed epitomized a deepened sense of the Church as a fortress besieged by the infidel modern world.

The chief defensive weapon in that beleaguered fortress was God's gift of infallibility to the pope, defined just before the Council dispersed. A long history lay behind that definition, though more and more it seems that its distinctive vocabulary belongs to the nineteenth century. In the later Middle Ages, discontent with the papacy had been articulated into the theories of conciliarism, whereby full authority lies with a General Council of all the bishops, summoned indeed by the pope, but where his opinions carry of themselves no decisive weight. A situation where the pope was first among equals naturally meant that the majority would resist any centralizing of spiritual power in a papal monarchy that could override contrary views. In particular, conciliarism favoured the right of any national Church to determine its own internal affairs. The later forms of this view were particularly associated with France and for that reason it was often called Gallicanism. By 1870 it formed part of the opposition to the 'ultramontane' element, who wished for greater concentration of authority over the whole Church in Rome 'beyond the mountains'. The situation was complicated by Pope Pius IX's own attiude. Originally of liberal outlook, he had been appalled by the anticlerical excesses of the Italian nationalists. The issue identifying church authority with the papacy was therefore bound up with opposition to political and intellectual liberalism.

The constitution *Pastor Aeternus* defined the pope's infallibility as an article of belief binding upon all the faithful. In fact it did little more than formalize the belief which most Catholics had long held. While it ruled out a strict Gallican theory, and several prominent leaders left the Catholic communion as a result, it so hedged about the occasions when the pope could speak infallibly that most could accept it. The pope was infallible only 'when he speaks *ex cathedra*, that is, in discharge of the office of pastor and teacher of all Christians, he defines a doctrine regarding faith or morals to be held by the Universal Church'.[53] The ultramontanes were disappointed by those limitations. The only occasion since 1870 when the power has been exercised was in 1950, when Pope Pius XII defined the assumption of the Blessed Virgin Mary.

In one respect at least the dogma of infallibility represented a clear victory for the ultramontanes. National churches had their wings well and truly clipped. Bishops were theoretically the full representatives of Christ in their sees, but a great many matters were reserved to Rome for the pope's decision, which meant in practice that of the appropriate curial department. The resultant bureaucracy developed the marks of its kind, its outlook being notably conservative. No more than any bureaucracy did it relish the disturbance of its even ways. Combine those attitudes with the general isolation of Catholicism from the scientific-humanist-secular outlook of the twentieth century, and the fortress is well-nigh impregnable. Any approach towards dialogue with non-Catholics of other religions or none will be seen as dangerous. Indeed, an open Catholic attitude even in marginal matters may prove a Trojan horse within the gates. So it was that the many Catholics, theologians and others, who in the years 1870–1960 tried to build bridges between the Church and the rest of the world, were liable to be suppressed in some appropriate way. Uniformity of worship, notably in the near-universal use of Latin as the language of the Mass, typified the monolithic appearance which Rome presented to the world. That uniformity found its ideal guardian in the Curia.

Small wonder, then, that Pope John XXIII's decision to call a General Council evoked no enthusiasm within the Curia. There was no need for such extravagance. But when the bishops assembled in Council they showed themselves collectively un-willing to accept the careful statements of the matters to be dis-cussed which the curial officials had prepared. Further, many scholars who had been working towards expressing the Catholic faith in ways which enabled genuine debate with non-Catholics were suddenly promoted from dangerous subversives to expert consultants. The documents produced by the Council were careful to contradict nothing essential to the teaching of Vatican I, but they set it in perspectives where matters that had seemed finally closed were opened for discussion and restatement.

Vatican I declared Catholic teaching on the authority of Peter's successor. Vatican II clarified – or began to clarify – it in relation to the authority of bishops, in their own right also apostolic successors.[54] The pope represents the universal

Church as a whole and also in each particular local church. The bishop also represents the one Church of Christ in the local church. It is not always easy to state the respective positions satisfactorily (nor indeed was it when Paul withstood Peter to the face at Antioch or confronted the Peter party at Corinth). The effect on the Curia has been mixed. The national hierarchies exercise wider discretion than they did before. But the greater the area of self-determination in different countries and cultures, the greater the risk that 'pluralism', a concept to be explored later, will become centrifugal to the point of schism. With uniformity in eclipse, a central bureaucracy is even more essential. The Curia was moderately reformed in 1967, when the Synod of Bishops was introduced as a theoretical counterpoise. Adjustment has proved especially difficult in two areas. The greater autonomy of national conferences of bishops has meant that the Catholic Church in a particular country has been able to define its attitude to many questions of local importance. In some cases the bishops have developed the suggestions of Vatican II for bringing the laity more fully into the making of appropriate decisions. Political coherence of this sort has not always agreed with the central policies of the Vatican, expressed through the papal diplomats. Relations have been difficult notably between the Vatican and the Church behind the Iron Curtain, where the papal policy has sometimes seemed unduly relaxed. The other problem area has been between university theologians and the Congregation for the Doctrine of Faith, of which more will be said later.

5

A Protestant attempt to discover the papacy is bound to start from the Protestant experience. It is the attempt to discern the meaning in something which is at once very close and very alien. It is possible to trace some of the features which made the Reformation far into the Middle Ages, finding this or that Reformation characteristic growing within the medieval unity; but not until the sixteenth century do Protestant bodies appear in deliberate, indeed exultant, independence of Rome. It is no far-fetched analogy to speak of Rome as the mother-church of the

West. In terms of the Church's historical geography, Protestant and Catholic stand together as Western.

The division between Eastern and Western Christendom is far older and more profound than the internal differences of the West. When the prayers have been answered and the heirs of the Reformation are reunited with Rome, the time will have come for an even greater ecumenical venture of faith, the restoration of full communion between Rome and the Eastern Orthodox Churches in communion with the Patriarch of Constantinople. And when all the heirs of Chalcedon are one, the way may open for those other ancient Churches to add their treasures to the total Christian unity. The scheme expresses the logic in the restoring of Christian unity. But to speak thus is to speak foolishly, in limited human fashion. The Holy Spirit who alone creates unity is not bound by the logic of any timetable. But it is wise to remember how much longer the schism between East and West has lasted than the internal divisions of the West.

The Great Schism cannot be dated very certainly. There was the occasion in 1054, when Cardinal Humbert, and his fellow papal legates excommunicated Michael Cerularius, Patriarch of Constantinople, and two colleagues: to be themselves excommunicated in return. In 1965, Pope Paul VI and the Patriarch Athenagoras solemnly lifted the anathemas of that day. But the events of 1054 were only the symptoms of a rift which began much earlier, which had developed largely in parallel with the growth of papal authority. The rift reached its ugliest dimensions in the Crusades, in particular in 1204 when the Western crusaders actually attacked Constantinople and the Western Church set up a Latin hierarchy in rivalry to the existing Byzantine one. Two hundred years later the Council of Florence achieved a reconciliation which proved quite hollow. Relations remained totally broken until the events which led to 1965. A new era has clearly begun, but a massive task remains.[55]

The jurisdictional quarrel ran and runs parallel with a theological difference, and that is probably to be traced to a deep cultural difference deriving from language and the different ways of understanding which each language suggests. The Western addition of the words 'and the Son' to the credal teaching on the Holy Ghost 'proceeding from the Father', previously agreed between East and West, happened almost accidentally. As 'the Filioque clause' it has become a rallying cry. Opinions differ over how profound or far-reaching a theological point is involved, and there is every hope that theologians studying the matter together across the East–West divide will go deep enough to find the way to agreement. But the Filioque clause involves other issues beside the strictly theological. These issues pass through the different genius of the Greek and Latin tongues. Greek is finely adapted to making precise distinctions over the inward essence of a matter. Latin, more robust, less subtle, more extrovert, perhaps is better suited to legal clarity than to metaphysical precision. But language is only one element in a delicate and complex network of assumptions and attitudes which the best words can express only clumsily, but which are experienced in the characteristic approaches to life and death, to the natural world, and to worship, of Eastern and Western Christians.

Relations between Orthodox Churches and the Anglican Churches have been, and are, varied. Nowadays, of course, quicker travel and greater mobility have at least breached the geographical isolation so that Greek and Russian communities are familiar in many English and American cities. But at the time of the Reformation those Churches were very exotic. The Greeks throughout the Levant were under Turkish domination, and the Turks were a crusading Muslim empire. The siege of Malta in 1563, followed by the Battle of Lepanto eight years later, checked their advance into mainland Europe, but as late as 1683 they laid siege to Vienna itself. England maintained good relations with the Turks, largely for reasons of trade, throughout the seventeenth century, with a diplomatic and commercial presence in Turkish lands. Some of the British residents established friendly relations with the local Christians, though Orthodox worship was a far cry from the Book of Common Prayer. Anglican theologians of the time, anxious to define their position between Rome and the Puritans, looked with interest at these episcopal churches which did not accept the Roman claims. Relations at times were cordial and interest reciprocal, though that was generally more for political than theological reasons. One Patriarch of Constantinople, Cyril

Lucar, was deeply influenced by Calvinist theology, but his views were never accepted in his own Church.

The Oxford Movement of the last century based its claim that the Church of England was a true part of the Catholic Church in part upon the Branch theory. The one, holy, catholic, and apostolic Church, tracing its descent by succession from the apostles, had come to exist in three main branches, the Roman, the Eastern, and the Anglican. Since Rome had, predictably, little time for this view, the cause of good relations with the Orthodox was stimulated. The prize most eagerly sought was Orthodox recognition of Anglican orders, whose validity the Roman Catholics continued to deny. The Ottoman Turkish Empire, long in decline, was finally ended in the First World War, with the consequent liberation of nationalities whose sense of identity had been preserved largely through their church membership. Perhaps more important to the growing contact between Anglicans and Orthodox was the Russian Revolution and its wave of Orthodox exiles. That there has been, and is, a strong element of ecclesiastical diplomacy in Anglican–Orthodox relations cannot be denied. Nor is that diplomacy onesided only, or exclusively ecclesiastical.

It would be a mistake to dismiss Anglican–Orthodox relations on a note of cynicism. Many treasures of spiritual insight have been shared and a healthy discontent stimulated which finds it intolerable to regard even the most ancient and cherished of barriers as permanent. But what to do about it is less obvious. There are those who maintain that, for example, intercommunion could properly be reached between Anglicans and Orthodox, rather on the model of that which has been introduced between Anglicans and Old Catholics. I do not see the cases as parallel. The Old Catholics, like the Anglicans, are a group which left the Roman Church; they belong alike to the Western tradition within Christendom. I believe that those Orthodox churchmen are wisest who wish to postpone full communion with the Anglicans until after the Anglicans have returned to full communion with Rome. The Anglican experience will then contribute to that fullness of Western tradition, and perhaps its greater completeness will make it easier to recover the unity which it shares with the East.

At a less ambitious level, however, Anglican contact with Orthodoxy has had far-reaching results. Eastern perspectives are different enough from the Western to enable Westerners who use them to see afresh some issue which in the West has become hopelessly snarled in controversy. Partly because of the basic difference in outlook, partly because the East has never been sundered by the typical Reformation disagreements, Orthodoxy can sometimes interpret Catholic to Protestant and vice versa. It was in this spirit that I appealed to Orthodoxy in *Mary and the Christian Gospel*, a book which aimed to break a Western deadlock by finding an attitude to the Lord's mother which would reconcile the essentials of Catholic teaching with the central impulses of Evangelical Christianity. Like many others, I had been awakened to the interpretative possibilities of Orthodoxy through the Fellowship of St Albans and St Sergius,[56] which for half a century has provided the setting for costly and rewarding ecumenical encounter. It is encouraging to find Professor Meyendorff and other Orthodox theologians defining Peter's primacy in terms of Orthodox tradition.[57]

One point in particular where the witness of Orthodoxy may prove of direct value to Western reunification is the system of patriarchates. Orthodoxy, it is stressed, has no monarchical pope. The several Churches of Orthodoxy are autocephalous. The area which each Church covers has usually been determined by political history so that a Church is conterminous with its nation. But in each separate Orthodox Church, the one holy orthodox catholic Church is present. Those Churches are defined by their communion with the Patriach of Constantinople, who is styled Oecumenical Patriarch.

The patriarchal system dates from before the breach between East and West. It is a means of preserving the unity of a worldwide Church that makes administrative sense without violating sacramental authority. From the sixth century, Patriarch was the title for bishops of the five chief sees, Rome, Alexandria, Antioch, Constantinople, and Jerusalem. Those bishops were responsible for areas much wider than their own see. They ordained the 'metropolitans' who were bishops in the centres of civil administration. Broadly speaking, the metropolitans in their turn exercised control over the bishops of smaller towns within their province.

The pope is, as he was anciently, Patriarch of the Western Church, and he is recognized as such by the Easterns. In the West, his universal jurisdiction as pope may be distinguished from his function as Patriarch of the Latin Church. Father Yarnold, s.j., and Professor Chadwick in their commentary on the Anglican–Roman Catholic International Commission report *Authority in the Church*, suggest that the Anglican Communion might find unity with Rome as a patriarchate in full communion with the Roman see. 'If intervention in an Anglican diocese were necessary, it would be made in the first instance by the Anglican primate; the bishop of Rome would step in only when all else had failed.'[58]

4
Implications

ECUMENICAL ATTITUDES

The Church can be described in many ways, especially when it is a body with a continuous history as long as that of the Church of Rome. I compared its beginnings with the primordial broth upon whose molecules the action of the sun produced life. On a Catholic understanding, the latest ingredient to become solid enough for its definitive shape to be seen is the papacy. Not that the process is yet complete. The First Vatican Council decided that under particular and restricted conditions the pope could speak for the Church without prior assent of the bishops. Vatican II showed more clearly the connection between pope and bishops. Administrative action and theoretical discussion since have brought further clarification and there is no doubt more to come.

The previous chapter described the Roman church from the outside. Aspects of its history and organization were selected in order to convey something of this many-sided institution which claims so much for itself in this world and beyond. The sheer size of the subject means that the selection can only be arbitrary; the result is not a portrait but an impression. The same will be true of the next stage of the inquiry, which is to go beneath the surface of the phenomenon and try to see from within why it is what it has become.

So far I have written as an historian or even a reporter. The Roman Catholic Church is a major historical institution which has shown surprising powers of enduring and adapting. It has outlasted the Roman Empire, medieval Christendom and the age of European colonialism. It has remained a local church, for its head has always (despite periods of exile) been bishop of Rome. In today's world of growing technological unity in culture, it is represented in every continent and nearly every country and, though neither the Eastern Churches nor the Anglican and Protestant bodies recognize its claim to be the one true Church of Christ, it is more than ever a force which Christian and secular opinion must take into account.

Historian, reporter, and sociologist are essential for identifying that which is making the claims. But their work cannot answer the fundamental question: are those claims true? Here we move into the theologian's province. And who, it may fairly be asked, is the theologian? The word should mean one who understands the ways of God. It is more often taken to mean an expert in what people have believed about God. The two overlap when the theological expert is a person of faith and commitment, of experienced as well as learned knowledge. The theologian in his learned work must not neglect the needs of the unlearned believer and may indeed be rebuked or enriched by the directness of unlearned experience of God. That is especially true of an ecumenical exploration into disputed theological territory.

Doing theology ecumenically demands an attitude best described by the word empathy. It means understanding not merely what those from whom we differ believe, but why they believe it; what it means to them; what the fact that we do not believe it means to them. In order to advance ecumenically we have to suspend our own disbelief for a moment, seeing to the limit of possibility the matter as it appears to their eyes. That does not mean that we commit ourselves in advance to a change of mind or of side. It means that we refocus and probably redefine the matter before considering afresh our own attitude towards it.

Empathy is seldom possible immediately. In matters of personal religious commitment there are obstacles to be overcome first. As John Wilkinson put it, 'we tend to develop a version of their doctrine which is not so much what they believe, as what we disbelieve'.[1] Accurate information helps to expose confusion, and the rest of this chapter aims to provide it. But there are other, less identifiable obstacles to empathy. I referred in the opening chapter to historical and social experiences which have virtually conditioned the English Protestant mind to react negatively in any discussion of the papacy. At more theological levels, there are words and notions in everyday Catholic use which trigger Protestant hostility. Merit, penance, tribunal, appeals, for example ring coldly. They sound legalistic, concerned with law rather than with the love that is at the heart of the gospel. The Latin origin of Catholic theology often translates into a bizarre English that is repellingly alien. The same is true of much Catholic devotion, especially perhaps at the theological periphery least influenced by the spirit of Vatican II. The doctrinal wall against the papal system is topped with forbidding cultural spikes.

The empathy needed to approach in an open spirit Catholic teaching on the papacy will be nourished by certain basic theological beliefs. The first of these concerns the Christian community. In the past, there has been a Catholic community and a Protestant community. There has been little sense that both were groups within a larger whole. It has been possible to view Catholic beliefs from outside, for they had nothing to do with us. There are parts of the world – Northern Ireland is the tragically obvious example – where this state of affairs still exists. But the last thirty years have seen a new and growing awareness that behind sectarian differences there stands a Christian community that embraces all who acknowledge Christ. The fact of being Christians together in a hostile world outweighs the differences between us.

If we belong to one community with all other Christians, we must be responsible for one another. 'If one member suffers, all suffer together; if one member is honoured, all rejoice together.'[2] St Paul's teaching on the one Body has taken new meaning. We cannot avoid responsibility for one another. If we believe one group of Christians to be in error, therefore, we may no longer throw up our hands in horror, rejoicing in our separated purity: 'Lord, I thank thee that we Protestants are not as these Catholics are.' We must realize that we are all implicated in the one-sided development that falls to the lot of Christian groups deprived of the strength that comes from unrestricted fellowship in the one Body. Our basic attitude should be: 'Lord,

have mercy on all us Christian sinners.' Community, responsibility, and penitence make the soil in which ecumenical
empathy can flourish.

They must be distinguished from the sentimentality which
may give a quick, even spectacular, growth, but which cannot
nourish a healthy plant. The demands of truth and integrity
remain. Penitence does not imply that we have been wrong in
our conclusions. It does demand that we should go into
disputed matters afresh with supple and humble intelligence. It
means that we cease protesting our own rightness and make the
attempt to grasp sympathetically as well as critically those
developments which we find antipathetic. Only when we have
listened with a mind that tries to accept are we in a position
responsibly to reaffirm our previous rejection.

Ecumenical theology is thus pursued by dialogue, and is
bound to be a costly business. It requires the engagement of
spiritual as well as intellectual powers and can hardly be done in
isolation from faith and prayer. 'Dialogue', I wrote in an essay
published in 1963, 'demands a degree of calmness, balance, and
dispassionate concern which is superhuman. . . . Our
theological differences must be examined in obedience to the
overriding prayer "Thy will be done." '[3] That, and the full
acceptance of the Christian integrity of those with whom one is
engaged in dialogue, remain essential.

2
THE CUMULATIVE QUALITY

The courtiers who surrounded Louis XVIII of France, it was
said, had forgotten nothing and learned nothing.[4] The first part
at least accounts for a feature prominent in the varied styles of
Roman Catholic theology, its cumulative quality. Nowhere is
this more apparent than in how the Church describes itself, particularly in the claims made for papal authority. Pope Paul's
Credo of the People of God, published in 1968, gives an excellent
example:

> We believe in one holy Catholic and Apostolic Church, built by
> Jesus Christ on the rock which is Peter. She is the Mystical Body of
> Christ, a visible society, hierarchically structured, and a spiritual

community – the Church on earth, the People of God on pilgrimage, the Church enriched with heavenly blessings, the germ and beginning of the Kingdom of God, through which the work and suffering of the Redemption are continued throughout human history, and which yearns for its perfect fulfilment at the end time in the glory of heaven. The Lord Jesus forms his Church through the sacraments which derive from his own plenitude. For she ensures that her members share in the mystery of the death and resurrection of Jesus Christ in the Grace of the Holy Spirit who gives her activity and life. . . .[5]

This Church is the guardian of that which God has revealed. Heir to the divine promises made to Israel,

> . . . the Church is built on the foundation of the Apostles. Their ever-living word and their pastoral powers she hands on faithfully in every century to the successors of Peter and to the Bishops in communion with him. The Holy Spirit unfailingly assists her. . . . We believe in the infallibility enjoyed by the successor of Peter when he speaks *ex cathedra* as shepherd and teacher of all the faithful, an infallibility which the whole Episcopate also enjoys when it exercises with him the supreme magisterium.[6]

The *Credo* was issued in 1968, designated a year of faith, and it was clearly meant as a stabilizing document in the heady years which followed Vatican II. The Pope's language skilfully picks up, echoes rather than quotes, and blends together the phrases used by his predecessors. 'Mystical Body of Christ', for instance, takes up the language of Pius XII in *Mystici Corporis Christi*, an encyclical of 1943 which marked a turning in post-Vatican I theology by enclosing juridical aspects of doctrine within the biblical view of the Church as the Body of Christ. Pius XII in so doing endorsed the studies of St Paul made by Catholic scholars over the previous generation. And in his own day Pope Pius had recalled Leo XIII in *Satis Cognitum*: 'By the very fact of being a body the Church is visible.' With the figure of the people of God on pilgrimage, however, Pope Paul moves decisively into the language of Vatican II, where that figure is the dominant image of the great dogmatic constitution *Lumen Gentium*. That emphasis is one which Protestant as well as Catholic can approve. But that does not mean abandoning the older, ecumenically unacceptable declarations of Vatican I, whose formulation of papal infallibility is echoed uncompromisingly, though with Vatican II's greater stress on the place of bishops.

Catholic theology is essentially cumulative. It is marked by continuity so that nothing which has once been declared true can later be declared false. But its context may be changed so that, seen in a new perspective, some consequences once assumed no longer apply, and others previously hidden come into prominence.

The Roman Catholic understanding of the Petrine function is thus a conviction that has developed with time. It is also one which may be expressed at very different levels of sophistication. The presentation of Catholic doctrine is much influenced by the audience to which it is addressed; that fact, obvious enough and sound commonsense, is nevertheless responsible for much irritation to Christians who stand outside. It is connected with the deep division between the teaching and the taught Church.

It is no doubt long history which has burned this distinction so deeply into the Catholic outlook. Almost from the moment that the Church left the shadows of persecution for the ambiguous light of state patronage, the twin problems of mass conversion and folk religion have existed. Semi-barbarian tribes in the aftermath of Empire accepted the faith. A Clovis was baptized and all his subjects with him. Few if any could read or write. Pope Gregory the Great sent out the monks to pioneer the Church in the pagan north; we noticed earlier his dealings with King Ethelbert.[7] The monks were essentially literate. Later, when letters were still a minority accomplishment, the priests were the clerks. Scholars in a medieval university were all in holy orders, a custom which outlasted the Reformation and applied to Fellows of colleges in Oxford and Cambridge until the mid-nineteenth century. The phenomenon of an educated laity is surprisingly new, and the Church is only beginning to see what it implies.

Liberated Catholic theologians of Vatican II and after pour scorn on the 'theology of the manuals', compendiums of the faith designed to be as succinct and memorable as possible. Covering dogmatics and moral theology, the more detailed of these works, often read in Latin, formed the staple until recent years of the parish priest's theological education. They gave summaries of the Church's doctrine backed by appropriate quotation from the Scripture and the Fathers, stock answers which spell out uncompromisingly Catholic truth against the unacceptable views of heretics. They are essentially functional works, basic textbooks. Shorter versions were adapted to the needs of Catholic teachers. 'It may be encouraging to the student', writes the author of one of the simpler ones, the Revd Charles Hart, 'to know that, at a recent examination in Religious Doctrine for teachers, the first place in all England was secured by one who had used no other work in preparing for the examination than *The Student's Catholic Doctrine*.'[8] The proud author wrote that in his preface to the eighteenth impression, made in 1943; the book was first published in 1916.

Father Hart reflects faithfully the teaching on papal authority declared at Vatican I, with no concessions to a critical or speculative approach; here was the information for those who wished to learn it. With his words 'Thou art Peter and on this rock . . .' Christ established that religious society, the Church, the Kingdom of God upon earth, of which Peter was to be the head. The equations are made without qualification.

> Now a Kingdom or State is necessarily composed of two orders of citizens, those who are to command, and those who are to obey. So too in God's Kingdom upon earth, we have those who are to command and teach, and those who are to obey and be taught. The first constitute the teaching and governing Church, and are composed of the Bishops and priests; the ordinary people, the laity, are the taught and governed.[9]

Father Hart's book is perhaps an extreme case. It is cited, not for ridicule, but because its wide circulation over a generation and more means that many Catholics will have learned their faith in the framework of attitudes which it displays. Among them will be many priests. It is hardly surprising that many are bewildered by the Catholicism which has emerged from Vatican II, with its emphasis upon a responsible laity who together with the hierarchy make up the people of God.

Hart was a schoolmaster-priest who wrote primarily for

colleges and prospective teachers and for private instruction. 'It is hoped, too,' he adds, 'that it will be found especially suitable to put into the hands of the intending convert.'[10] The training of the clergy naturally called for a larger work where the conclusions would be supported by detailed arguments and authorities. One of the finest works in this category is Ludwig Ott's *Fundamentals of Catholic Dogma*.[11] First published in 1952, it is recent enough to have taken into account Pope Pius XII's encyclical *Mystici Corporis Christi* and the earlier phase of the revival in biblical studies which that pope cautiously encouraged. But although it belongs to the last years before Vatican II, its method in organizing the material remains faithful to the spirit of Vatican I.

Dr Ott's treatment of the Church forms the second part of his fourth book, 'The Doctrine of God the Sanctifier'; the first part set forth the doctrine of grace. The first chapter on the divine origin of the Church considers the concept 'Church' itself, the founding of the Church by Christ and the purpose of the Church. The second chapter, which concerns us most, is on the constitution of the Church. Six sections deal with its hierarchical nature, the primacy of Peter, the primacy of the pope's jurisdiction, the nature of papal primacy, infallibility, and the bishops. Chapter 3 relates the inner constitution of the Church to Christ and the Holy Spirit. Chapter 4 rehearses the 'properties or essential attributes' of the Church, which means indefectibility, infallibility, and visibility as well as the four traditional 'notes' of the Church: one, holy, catholic, and apostolic. Chapter 5 emphasizes the necessity of the Church and of belonging to it while the last chapter treats of the communion of saints. The third part of Book Four is devoted to the sacraments.

Dr Ott thus presents a highly integrated, systematic statement of the faith. If you want to know how Catholicism was taught and what Catholicism taught in the years before Vatican II disturbed the newly traditional certainties, you will find it here. But the book is of more than historical value, a foil to the theologians of today. Ott's connections between one aspect of the faith and another give much food for thought. Comparison between his treatment of a theme and the more open-ended handling by a theologian of the nineteen-seventies does not always favour the latter.

A clue worth following by anyone seeking from the outside to reach the distinctive inwardness of traditional Catholic teaching is the system of grading items of church teaching, with correspondingly graded obligations to believe. Ott sets them out clearly.[12] The highest grade is that of immediately revealed truth, *fides divina*, vouched for by infallible teaching authority (*fides catholica*). When truths of this order have been solemnly defined by pope or General Council, they are said to be *de fide definita*. A like authority attaches to the second category of Catholic truths or church doctrines which are formally taught without being 'immediately revealed truths'. The third grade is that of *sententia fidei proxima*, 'teaching proximate to faith', which is very generally taught by the best authorities though not formally promulgated. The fourth grade, *sententia theologice certa*, is a doctrine whose truth follows from that of another which is *de fide definita*. The fifth, 'common teaching', is a doctrine which while generally accepted is still a free option, and it shades off into the sixth, 'pious opinions' on undefined matters which may be rated probable, more probable, or well-founded. Dr Ott ends his formidable analysis with a welcome note: not all the assertions of the Church's teaching authority on questions of faith and morals are infallible and therefore irrevocable.

This grading is, of course, based upon the Church as its teaching emerged from the First Vatican Council. The Second Vatican Council embodied most of its teaching in this field in the dogmatic constitution on the Church, *Lumen Gentium*.[13] Comparison between the perspective shown there and that of Ludwig Ott is instructive. The Vatican II document starts by considering the mystery of the Church under a variety of images found in the New Testament: sheepfold, tillage (1 Corinthians 3.9), building, mother and bride, new creation, body: each of them understood to suggest ways in which Christ's saving work continues. Chapter 2 develops the theme 'people of God', taken to be the master-image. Only in chapter 3 is the hierarchical constitution of the Church considered. This chapter, which has been criticized for a juridical emphasis out of keeping with the others, deliberately starts from Vatican I, to whose teaching it introduces a new stress on the 'collegiality' of bishops, among whom Peter and his successors have the prime place. Bishops appear almost an afterthought in Ott's treatment. But Vatican II has freed itself from the fear of Gallicanism which so conditioned Vatican I, and can therefore consider bishops more adequately.

The laity are treated of far more generously than used to be the case. *Lumen Gentium* devotes chapter 4 to their place in the Church. No doubt it is the prior stress on the Church as people of God which insists that the laity 'in their own way share in the priestly, prophetic, and kingly office of Christ, and to the best of their ability carry on the mission of the whole Christian people in the Church and in the world.'[14] The basic distinction so stressed by Father Hart is still present, but interpreted in a different spirit: 'Like all Christians, the laity should promptly accept in Christian obedience what is decided by the pastors who, as teachers and rulers of the Church, represent Christ.'[15] But the pastors for their part 'should recognize and promote the dignity and responsibility of the laity . . .' and 'willingly use their prudent advice . . .'[16]

Catholic teaching on Peter's place in the Church may thus be expressed in many different styles. Some of the differences are simply matters of presentation, a sensible shaping of material for the particular readership intended. But there are also deeper differences. Views which are deemed *de fide* do not change, but they may come to look different when they are seen in a new perspective. Father Hart's popular presentation and Dr Ott's more learned approach reflect alike a concern to express the Catholic faith in contrast to Protestant and other views. *Lumen Gentium* presents the same positions equally without compromise, but avoids unnecessary differences with other Christians by advancing towards the distinctively Roman doctrines from positions which most other Christians could accept. Pope Paul's *Credo* has been criticized by Catholics who wish to go further along the paths opened up by Vatican II,[17] but it in no way goes back on *Lumen Gentium*. It is interesting also to note that the widely advertised correspondence course published in London by the Catholic Enquiry Centre[18] follows closely the order of *Lumen Gentium* when, in the fourth booklet, it comes to deal with the Church.

It should now be clear that there are considerable differences in the presentation of the Catholic faith before and after the Second Vatican Council. It should also be clear that, despite the hopes of some Protestants and the fears of some Catholics (and perhaps also the fears of some Protestants and the hopes of some Catholics), the difference lies in the presentation of the faith, not in its content. Older and newer presentations share the same basic convictions and make the same basic assumptions about the proper nature of Christian faith. Those assumptions are not always perceived by Protestants trying to engage in dialogue. The next few chapters will attempt to identify some of the more important.

3
CONTINUITY AND CHANGE

The notion of continuity during historical change is fraught with possibilities for misunderstanding, but it is central to the Catholic understanding of the Church.

One result of the sudden acceleration during the last century of human control over the environment was a new interest in time and its meaning. Two interpretations of time formulated at the period are specially important in the study of theological institutions, and their implications need to be carefully distinguished. Charles Darwin is chiefly associated with the evolutionary view whereby species develop by changing. Natural selection ensures that only the fittest survive, which means that the latest and best renders obsolete the less successful type from which it evolved. Darwin's contemporary, John Henry Newman, propounded the theory of development, according to which the later forms of the Christian faith, where they are authentic, represent the unfolding or elucidation of that which was present in germ from the start. Both views express the modern awareness of transience and have contributed to the 'historical' approach which prevails in most branches of learning. 'Evolution' was advanced as a way of understanding the development of species, and 'development' used to show the inner continuity of Catholic teaching; but both terms have been taken over into the common stock of twentieth-century attitudes, so that we speak indifferently of the evolution or development of the motor car or of the social services.

Professor C. F. D. Moule has called attention to the profound difference between the two conceptions when they are applied to the origin of Christology.[19] The use of historical methods suggests that some of the ways in which the New Testament speaks about Jesus are older than others, and that after New Testament times church doctrine about Christ built on the later rather than the earlier forms. Recent studies of the matter have tended to interpret it on evolutionary lines so that when the new form is established, the old is discarded. Dr Moule prefers a developmental model. 'But if, in my analogy, "evolution" means the genesis of successive new species by mutations and natural selection along the way, "development", by contrast, will mean something more like the growth, from immaturity to maturity, of a single specimen from within itself.'[20]

Now Catholics claim that the relation between Peter and the papacy is one of development, not evolution. There is a distinctive pastoral function which was first seen in St Peter, and which has since been exercised through his successors in the papacy. The differences between the fisherman-shepherd and the pontiff of the Middle Ages, the Renaissance, or today suggests from the outside at most an evolutionary connection between successive distinct species. But that is not the case. Protestants greet the Catholic claim with scepticism. They need to be convinced that Peter may be discerned within the papacy. Do the layers of history and pomp and statecraft peel away to reveal at the centre the Galilean features of the fisherman-shepherd? Or do they, like Peer Gynt's onion, continue peeling until there is no centre at all?

This book is neither the first nor the last to grapple with the problem. It has the advantage of following an already large body of fruitful ecumenical study which has replaced rigid confrontation of older polemics. In particular, the concept of 'Petrine ministry' has provided a category which can relate the New Testament evidence to the historical existence of the papacy without the need for prior agreement on historical continuity, in an area where the evidence is notoriously inconclusive. 'Petrine ministry', to be sure, is not a synonym for 'papacy'. Petrine ministry means that sort of service which Peter rendered to the founding generation of the Church. Rome claims the Petrine succession, but it would be possible to maintain that there is a Petrine ministry which Rome should be exercising but which has been so abused in the papacy that it cannot be recognized. Alternatively, it is possible to recognize a Petrine ministry quite unconnected with any lasting primacy at Rome.

Many Protestants assume that the whole enterprise of identifying a permanent Petrine ministry within the Church is mistaken. Peter was one of the original chosen twelve disciples, the apostle upon whose labours the Church was founded, the first even among the apostles. Yet in himself he belonged entirely to the first generation and his later importance is confined to the part which the Scriptures show him to have played. In any case, it was his faith that was important, not himself. There is no particular succession of apostles. The institution which Peter and his colleagues founded, or stabilized, is in itself of no value. Its constitution, organization, and any other administrative detail are points of indifference. All that matters is for there to be a succession of believers who will carry forward the spirit of Jesus into every human generation. Christians may organize themselves into one Church or many denominations or self-governing local churches as they please. The medium is not the message and church order is theologically indifferent. It becomes wrong only when institutional concerns absorb time and energy better spent on matters more central to the true Christian spirit.

This view represents the 'common sense' approach of many lay people. But it had no part in the original Protestant movement. Theologically, it belongs to the liberal phase of historic Protestantism when the strong Reformation themes were in decay. It is hardly to be found until the rationalist approach of the eighteenth century played down all but the ethical aspects of Christianity. Institutional factors then seemed to be no more than the scaffolding round the building itself, which was the Christian way of life. The pietist movement which countered rationalism in Germany and spread to England with the

Methodists and other Evangelicals was equally indifferent to church order, which did little to warm the heart. A contrast between spirit and institution runs through the various forms of liberal Christianity. Peter is interesting only as an historical character or as an object lesson in discipleship.

The historic Protestant tradition has continued to exist alongside its liberal derivatives. A high view of doctrine allows the traditional Protestant to hold firm convictions about the Church and its structures. The arrangements of the apostolic age are a proper guide for the later Church. But the traditional Protestant parts company with the Catholic in seeing a gulf between the New Testament time and all later ages. Thus the apostolic succession is a matter of keeping the apostles' doctrine as it is preserved in Scripture. Looking at the Church as the New Testament shows it to have been, they note the conflict between Paul and the Judaizers over whether Gentile converts should be circumcised. They find it to be an example of a pattern that recurs throughout the history of the Church. The Reformation saw the freedom of the gospel asserted against the 'Judaizing' tendencies of the medieval Church, with its emphasis on religious practices (not to mention payments) as the way of salvation. True apostolic succession was regained when Martin Luther rediscovered the power of the apostolic gospel. Genuinely apostolic church order was that which provided a discipline in which gospel freedom could be nurtured.

The old Church of England Book of Common Prayer provided such a discipline for a comprehensive Christian state. The traditional church order of a threefold ministry was maintained and Bishop Jewel,[21] the chief apologist for the Elizabethan Settlement, insisted that it was more faithfully continued under Canterbury than in Rome, where alien elements had been allowed to confuse and befoul the purest traditions of the apostles. Those English reformers who chiefly defined the Anglican Church insisted that, while the Scriptures alone gave the rule of faith, those Scriptures were rightly interpreted by the Creeds, the early Councils, and the consensus of teaching given by the accredited Fathers. It was a consequence of this insistence that the Scriptures should be interpreted within the great church tradition that in the seventeenth century a few most firmly

Anglican writers found it possible to speculate on a place for the pope in a rightly reformed Church.[22]

Nevertheless, the gap remained. Anglicans were as firm as other Protestants that the Bible remained the standard by which the acceptability of later developments should be measured. Apostolic succession meant succession in the doctrine of the apostles as set out in Scripture, not apostolic ministry as a living force transmitted by the laying-on of hands from one generation to the next, desirable and indeed normal as that church practice undoubtedly was.

Among the most interesting developments in Protestant theology of late has been the careful analysis of key biblical words and concepts. Kittel's great *Word Book of the Bible*,[23] though not beyond criticism for some of its presuppositions and methods,[24] is an indispensable tool for biblical scholars. Among the concepts studied, naturally, have been church, authority, apostleship. Oscar Cullmann made free use of K. L. Schmidt's[25] article on the Church and K. H. Rengstorff's[26] on apostleship for his study of Peter. He followed them in concluding that the apostolate, strictly speaking, belonged wholly to the first generation, that of the individuals who had been chosen to provide first-hand testimony to the resurrection. In the nature of the case that could not be repeated, so the apostolate could not be a permanent office in the Church. A Dutch Reformed writer, Norval Geldenhuys, used the same argument to show that the unique authority given to the apostles was for laying the foundation of the Church by their unique witness to the resurrection. That authority was preserved for posterity not in any particular ministerial order but in 'the canonical New Testament clothed with the authority of the Lord and his apostles'.[27] Geldenhuys' book has been curiously neglected. It uses the techniques of critical biblical study to reinstate the traditional Protestant position. If his conclusions be accepted it is pointless to expect a Peter factor in the Christian ministry.

A third group would probably consider the enterprise of discovering Peter in the papacy to be misleading as well as futile. They are the 'eschatological Protestants', by which awkward term I mean those who stress the radical discontinuity between Jesus and the subsequent church understanding of him. It was

73

Albert Schweitzer who exploded for ever the prevailing Protestant view that Jesus, stripped of the metaphysical and miraculous glory with which the bigoted devotion of early Catholicism had inappropriately clothed him, embodied the liberal ideals of the later nineteenth century. Schweitzer deployed the same techniques as the liberal Protestants to show that Jesus stood in the tradition of those Old Testament prophets who saw salvation only in a divine intervention suspending or terminating the process of human history. He was different from other apocalyptic prophets in believing himself to be the human instrument of that divine intervention. His death, a ransom for the guilt of his people, was to be the means and the moment for God's Kingdom to break through. So Jesus went up to Jerusalem in order to die.

> Jesus . . . in the knowledge that he is the coming Son of Man lays hold on the wheel of the world to set it moving on that revolution which is to bring all ordinary history to a close. It refuses to turn, and he throws himself upon it. Then it does turn, and crushes him. Instead of bringing in the eschatological conditions, he has destroyed them. . . .[28]

Schweitzer's interpretation is as arbitrary in its own way as those which he criticized and his reconstruction of Jesus has had few takers. A Swiss scholar, Martin Werner, was an exception, and he used Schweitzer's position to show how grossly early Catholicism had distorted the witness to Jesus.[29] In retrospect Schweitzer's view is one of many which drove a wedge between the Jewish outlook of the Gospels, or at least of the traditions at their root, and the Hellenistic notions which shaped the gospel message as it moved away from its Jewish origins. That the Church misunderstood Jesus is widely believed today. A less dramatic form of Schweitzer's reconstruction fits in with the opinion that, where Jesus cut across history, the Church came to terms with it. Much social criticism of the Church assumes that Jesus taught a lifestyle that was radically 'alternative'; but the Church has compromised with the world.

That judgement has gained ground lately. Catholics as well as Protestants have constructed theologies of liberation which, interpreting the gospel as political action, attack those who insist on the gospel's capacity to be at home in societies that resist revolutionary change. It has also been revived by some of the radical theologians who believe that the traditional doctrines of Christianity are no longer tenable. One of the most notable recent exponents of such a view is Don Cupitt, who achieved wide fame in 1977–8 by his contributions to *The Myth of God Incarnate*[30] and through his appearances on television.

For Mr Cupitt, the Christian betrayal of Jesus centred on the reconciliation between the transcendent, eschatological teaching of Jesus and the continued flow of history. A series of compromises drew the teeth of the authentic challenge which the Hebrew experience of God threw down before all human systems of religion. Mr Cupitt lays much of the blame at the door of the blasphemous urge to worship Jesus, which cannot avoid infringing the unique transcendence of the Lord Jehovah by 'humanizing' him. Any image of God comes under the hammer of Exodus 20.4. It also destroys the humanity of Jesus. The movement for the doctrinal clarification of God as Trinity and of Christ as his Son, the Word who took flesh in Jesus, was disastrous: from Nicaea to Chalcedon is a rake's progress. Further distortions occurred when the Empire became Christian, for Christ was represented as universal cosmic Emperor, with the earthly emperor his servant and vicar; indeed 'the entire imperial cult and ideology was refocused on Christ, while in return Christ crowned his earthly deputy and validated his rule'.[31] The conspiracy between theology and art reached a point where 'almost the only remaining trace of Jesus is his dark bearded semitic face, peering out with understandable sadness from its incongruous new setting'.[32] Christendom, the medieval climax of these trends, was the grave of Christianity; and only when the doctrine of incarnation is discarded can there be hope of resurrection.

Such views can have no time for finding Peter amid the ambiguities of the Vatican. Yet, formidable as it seems, I believe the challenge from eschatological Protestantism to be the least important of the three. Schweitzer, we saw, exploited the element of eschatology in the New Testament to expose the vacuity of liberal Protestant lives of Jesus. Unfortunately that admirable work of demolition was not followed by anything more constructive. But it is easier nowadays to take seriously the eschatological element in Jesus's teaching, giving it due weight within an overall understanding of doctrinal development which stresses continuity rather than discontinuity between apostolic times and the Church of the Fathers.

Mr Cupitt stands within a long Protestant tradition of distrusting the Hellenistic categories of thought in which those Fathers teased out the implications of the faith they had received. I believe, however, that it was in the divine plan for the faith to break out of the Jewish matrix in which alone it could have been forged. It had to be re-expressed in terms which opened it up as a faith for all mankind. Otherwise it would have run out into the sands as a revivalist Jewish sect. Further, the opposition to the new faith from pagan intellectuals shows how far it was from losing its identity in a mish-mash of philosophical speculation.[33] In any case, there would surely have been opposition voiced from within the Church against any serious distortion. Writings that have survived from before the Council of Nicaea are few and very different from each other. They have much to say about heresies, which they detect by comparison with a standard of faith that is strikingly consistent from one place to another; and its keynote is continuity with the teaching of the apostles.

Christianity reconstructed in the following of Schweitzer is so different from the traditional version that it is better regarded as an alternative religion. Unlike traditional Protestantism, which aimed to correct abuses in a system basically sound, it supposes a corruption so early and so widespread that for 1900 years all mainline church teaching grossly misunderstood its central figure. The Church, so far from being the guardian of truth, was its consistent enemy. This 'radical' alternative may or may not provide a religion attractive to modern man. It should not be confused with Christianity.

The same might be said of liberal Protestantism in some of its more extreme forms. We must distinguish here between two religious approaches which use almost the same technique. The faithful church member who goes to the New Testament, more particularly to the Gospels, and finds there sayings of Jesus or incidents featuring him which provide a personal inspiration for

Christian living is doing something different from the would-be theologian who declares that those same episodes are the only ones to express the authentic Jesus, and that all others must be judged by conformity to them. The first person is following a personal 'way' of devotion which may lead him into fuller discipleship. The second is attempting to define the faith according to the limits of his own belief.

Church history sadly shows many cases of devout Christians starting in the first position but moving on to the second. In the earlier years of the Reformation, when the sense of institution was stronger, an attractive teacher elevated his own devotion to the point where he and his followers formed their own sect around it. In some cases a succession of teachers ensured the continuance of a new denomination. In the Catholic Church a similar impulse of devotion might well have nourished a religious order or secular institute, continuing to strengthen and be strengthened by the wider body of which, despite occasional strain, it remained an obedient member.

More recently the pattern has varied. People have been satisfied with keeping their devotions to themselves. A liberal climate has nurtured the belief that tolerance is the queen of virtues. A person's religion is his own affair and, so long as it does not infringe the rights of others, it is no concern of anyone else. When Christian faith is a matter of individual devotion and Christian life is summed up in the maxim 'Do as you would be done by', there is no obvious need for an institutional Church. The Church may indeed have social functions in fostering the local community, as a pressure group or resource centre for humanitarian concerns which transcend or cut across local advantage, and as an emotional registrar providing rites of passage for family life. But religiously, the Church's chief function is to strengthen personal devotion. Should you find that the Church of your allegiance so far does not serve that purpose, you may well shop around until you find one that does, or you may simply cease to go to church at all. It has no bearing on your integrity as a Christian.

Liberal Christianity of that kind moves in a different world from the Catholic Church, whether that be located in Rome, Eastern Orthodoxy, or in the strong Reformation confessions.

For its sixteenth-century counterparts were not the Lutheran, Reformed, or Anglican Churches, but the many smaller sects which subordinated external authority in doctrine, in morals, and in church order to the inner light, to the direct guidance of the Spirit, to revelation in conscience and reason.

Liberal Christianity departs from the historic faith at the point where the spirit and institution are so contrasted that they mutually exclude each other: faith and love, the Spirit, and personal relationships pitted against hierarchy, sacraments, and liturgy. It must, of course, be admitted that the institutional Church has often provoked opposition by its bigoted actions, its tyranny in the realm of the spirit. But to condemn institutional Christianity as such because of its aberrations is as unrealistic as to condemn all individual spiritual experience as fanatical delusion. Some spiritual religion is evidently crazed, but that does not affect the possibility of genuine interior religion.

An issue of fact stands behind these considerations. Did Jesus teach a simple message of personal faith uncluttered with institutional concerns? The Liberals classically thought that he did, but their view is hard to sustain. His teaching has been preserved only through the institution which claims that he founded it. Much of that teaching was given specifically to the disciples in a manner which suggests that those disciples were not simply a group of individuals separately drinking in his teaching. They were a tight-knit group with their own customs, their common purse, even perhaps their pecking order. They were a flock and he their shepherd, a carefully disciplined type of association. The Acts of the Apostles shows that their discipline included strict accountability.[34] Even when they had been rejected by the principal authorities in contemporary Judaism, they stressed their identity with the community of Israel. That indeed lay very deep in their corporate self-awareness. Jesus was celebrated as Christ, the Messiah; but 'what is a Messiah without a messianic community?'[35]

Parallel to the myth of Christianity's institution-free start is the notion that what began simple and open and free was later complicated and enclosed in the toils of an ecclesiastical machine. In an unforgettable passage Evelyn Waugh describes his own enlightenment on this point:

I had sometimes thought it an odd thing that Western Christianity, alone of all the religions of the world, exposes its mystery to every observer, but I was so accustomed to this openness that I had never before questioned whether it was an essential and natural feature of the Christian system.

He mentions the common assumption of a journey from simplicity into complication. His experience at a Coptic Mass in Ethiopia showed the opposite to be true:

At Debra Lebanos I suddenly saw the classic basilica and open altar as a great positive achievement, a triumph of light over darkness consciously accomplished, and I saw theology as the science of simplification by which nebulous and elusive ideas are formalized and made intelligible and exact. I saw the Church of the first century as a dark and hidden thing; as dark and hidden as the seed germinating in the womb; legionaries off duty slipping furtively out of barracks, greeting each other by signs and passwords in a locked upper room in the side street of some Mediterranean seaport; slaves at dawn creeping from the grey twilight into the candle-lit, smoky chapels of the catacombs. The priests hid their office, practising trades; their identity was known only to initiates; they were criminals against the law of their country. And the pure nucleus of the truth lay in the minds of the people, encumbered with superstitions, gross survivals of the paganism in which they had been brought up; . . . And I began to see how these obscure sanctuaries had grown, with the clarity of Western reason, into the great open altars of Catholic Europe, where Mass is said in a flood of light, high in the sight of all, while tourists can clatter round with their Baedekers, incurious of the mystery.[36]

The most serious objections to a genuinely Petrine papacy come from historic Protestantism. It is to be rejected not as part of a deeper misunderstanding, but because its particular concentration of Christ's authority upon one person unbalances the great tradition which it purports to safeguard. This opposition is maintained with minor differences by Eastern Orthodox, Anglicans, Lutherans, and Reformed; as well as by the Old Catholics who at several stages since the Counter-Reformation, and particularly since the dogma of 1870, have rejected the

79

Roman claim. I shall argue, however, that the traditional faith for which they all stand is advanced, not distorted, by recognizing the Petrine office.

4
THE AUTHORITY OF DOCTRINE

The quality of the Christian faith as given, as a body of teaching, is as necessary for a Catholic understanding as its continuity; and this, too, has of late been widely disputed. Although the principal Protestant churches still for the most part officially subscribe to the beliefs which marked their original independent stand, those standards may play little part in the beliefs of ordinary church members, and many accredited ministers sit light to them also.

In 1976 the Doctrine Commission of the Church of England published its report under the title *Christian Believing*.[37] Its terms of reference had been 'the nature of the Christian Faith and its expression in Holy Scripture and Creeds', but, as the title implies, the theologians involved, a team who well represented the spectrum of English Anglican opinion, could only produce an agreed statement on what is involved in the act of believing. The content of belief is left to a series of essays, many of high value, which are the responsibility of each separate author only. In this there is a striking contrast with the last comparable volume, the report of the Commission on Christian Doctrine appointed in 1922, whose report was not published until 1938.[38] It was possible then for a group of Anglicans who represented all the main varieties of educated opinion to produce an agreed statement of the content of belief. Forty years later it was not possible, presumably, to do so in a worthwhile manner. The principal value of the 1976 report, as distinct from the individual contributions, lies in the sensitive analysis of what believing today involves.

A point especially worthy of note for the state of doctrine in the Church of England today is that what was previously considered the strength of the Christian faith now seems to be an embarrassment: its emphasis on history. The relation between today's believers and the 'deposit of faith' to which church allegiance commits them is complex and dialectical. The past is totally, irrevocably past; indeed, it appears, too far past to be of much use for the present. The series of essays by individual members of the Commission shows the wide diversity of belief among sophisticated Anglicans, as well as the bewildering variety of topics which they deem to be of the first importance.

The Commission is particularly interesting in the matter of creeds and their status. In an appendix, Professor Geoffrey Lampe attributes the origin of creeds to the need for Christians to identify themselves in face of spurious teachings which to the unwary sounded healthy. Although the ancient belief that the apostles agreed upon the creed called after them before departing on their several missions is a later invention, the view that a creed is a recognition signal is basically true. Short credal formulae are to be found in the earlier parts of the New Testament – 'No man can say that Jesus is Lord but by the Spirit'; and the Pastoral Epistles contain longer phrases which look very like embryonic creeds. The earliest formulae keep as far as possible to biblical words. But experience in the second and third centuries showed that straight Bible words and phrases could be used in more than one sense, and the pressures of controversy obliged the upholders of what rapidly became orthodox Catholic belief to use non-biblical expressions. 'Being of one substance with the Father' is one which was taken into the heart of orthodox belief.

The problem facing modern Christians is: are we permanently committed to phrases enshrining the outlook and philosophy of the fourth century? Until lately the problem has been nothing like so acute. But today's world view is vastly different from that of the fourth century; or from that of the sixteenth, when the Thirty-Nine Articles defined the teaching of the English Reformation; or, for that matter, of the first century when it all began. Limiting the question to the creeds – Apostles' Creed, Nicene Creed as included in Anglican worship – we must ask what authority they should have for today. The Doctrine Commission distinguished four main types of answer currently found in the Church of England, though it recognized that there were others.

The first group are those for whom the creeds remain the

norm of belief, the authentic interpretation of the biblical data. The creeds ring true to these people for, as well as signalling continuity of belief with the past, they express for today the standing beliefs concerning Christ. 'These Christians emphasize the givenness of the biblical witness both to God and to Christ who is its climax, and they joyfully discern in the creeds a faithful echo of this testimony and a true delineation of their incarnate Saviour and Lord.'[39] Such believers do not suppose that the credal statements exhaust the meaning of the mystery, but they are true pointers to what lies beyond words. It is essential therefore that the creeds should be maintained intact, though paraphrases of some kind may be desirable and useful. But whatever experimental forms may be required to communicate the truth to the present age, that truth remains the same and the historic creeds stand as yardsticks by which the adequacy of any new forms must be judged.

The second group is more modestly traditionalist. Its members have difficulties over particular clauses of the creed, either on their own account or because of doubts whether the Virgin Birth, for instance, represents adequately the original belief. But in general they go along with the creeds, and are happy to recite them as an act of solidarity with Christians past and present. Forms of words, they believe, are at best a limited means of expressing the unity between God and man to which they refer.

The third group stress the degree to which the creeds are conditioned by a vanished culture. These people can neither affirm nor deny the creeds, and most of them are unhappy about the place which they continue to hold in worship. But for the most part they do not wish to devise replacements. Their allegiance is less to the Church's faith as traditionally understood than to 'the continuing Church of God' which is perhaps not best served by precise descriptions of its beliefs.

The fourth group consists of those 'for whom the essence of the faith is to be found in a life of discipleship rather than in credal affirmation'.[40] Creeds for them belong wholly to the past, where they performed a useful negative service by shutting off blind alleys of belief. But they are hopelessly inadequate for communicating the reality they indicate; nor would any other

credal form do better. 'Such people do make theological affirmations but they do so by their lives and through their prayers.'

> They commit themselves to the Reality whom men call God as their
> creator, their saviour, and their sanctifier; and they commit
> themselves also to a life of Christian discipleship in the sense of
> loyalty to Jesus and to his values, attitudes, and teaching as depicted
> in the Gospels. They find in him a key to the truth about God and the
> world, and an authentic way of life. Commitment to God and to
> Jesus, understood in this sense, is more important to them than
> 'provisional' assent to credal propositions of any kind.[41]

The report realizes that these approaches make uneasy
bedfellows. Flat contradictions rule out a synthesis. But none of
the four must be disallowed. The Church must hold adherents
of them all in the one body, looking for a tension between them
which will be 'fruitful': 'not a state of non-communication
between mutually embattled groups but one of constant
dialogue with consequent cross-fertilization of ideas and insights'.[42] That happy condition is possible because the dialogue
takes place within a community of faith, sustained by mutual
prayer; because it concerns the proper way of holding an objective tradition which all sides share and to which they all make
reference; and because genuine dialogue is open to truth from
whatever quarter, from other churches, other religions, or 'any
authentic human discipline'.[43]

Dialogue is indeed essential to avoid polarization. At this
point the argument of *Christian Believing* runs very close to that of
the American Jesuit Avery Dulles in his account of the Roman
Catholic Church in the United States during the years following
Vatican II.[44]

In their sensitive analysis of the types of believing currently
found among educated Anglicans, the Doctrine Commission
brought to light a factor shared by all except the first group: the
assumption that a theological statement is true if it accords with
experience. If it does not 'light up', it is of no great consequence
except as a historical monument. This assumption goes back to
Coleridge's classic phrase '. . . whatever *finds* me, bears witness
for itself that it has proceeded from a Holy Spirit . . .'[45] and
expresses a vital constituent in true religion; but its negative

corollary is most unfortunate. It is closely related to the view that religious conviction, or opinion, is at its deepest a private matter where the ultimate arbiter is my moral or spiritual awareness. Here the exemplar is Coleridge's contemporary, Lord Melbourne, who is said to have exclaimed, after hearing an evangelical sermon, 'Things have come to a pretty pass when religion is allowed to invade the sphere of private life.'[46]

An extreme case, of course, but its cause lies deep. Evangelical religion, like other varieties of the historic faith, is authoritative. It persuades, it convinces, it demands. At its best it is an objective declaration of the actions and will of God with the consequent demand for obedience. It claims to inform both mind and conscience. Many beside Lord Melbourne have resented its pressure. They were not invariably wrong. The line between informing mind and conscience and violating both is easily crossed; it is a small step from persuasion to brainwashing.

Yet mind and conscience require informing. The resistance roused in many Christian people by 'being told what to do' may derive from the belief, formulated or not, that there is no authority outside the individual conscience. There is widespread hostility today to the notion of theology as an objective, given body of knowledge which God has revealed. The idea of the Church continuing across the generations as the divinely authorized custodian of this knowledge, is correspondingly unpopular. So is the notion of right and wrong in matters of belief, the idea that an orthodoxy exists independently of whether or not I find it acceptable. Resistance heightens into indignation when the belief in question seems to have no immediate practical consequences. Reactions of this kind build up into an attitude which cuts across all levels of theological sophistication. An anti-dogmatic temper in religious matters is particularly common among Anglo-Saxons.

Certainly it is found among Protestants. Louis Bouyer traces its growth in his book *The Spirit and Forms of Protestantism*.[47] A former Protestant pastor who became a priest of the Paris Oratory, Bouyer understood from inside the positive dynamic of both Luther and Calvin, whose main concerns he readily accepts to have been properly Catholic, though sadly muffled in the Catholic Church of the day: the freedom of grace, the priority of God's glory, and the sovereign authority of Scripture. Unfortunately the positive affirmations were weighted with negations. The priority of grace was so rigidly kept apart from all human effort that the Christian could never become in himself what he was in God's sight; justification remained extrinsic, the clothing with righteousness of one who himself remained foul. Similarly the stress on God's glory and sovereignty came to mean 'the crushing down of man, the non-existence, the impossibility, the total undesirability of any activity on his part which might claim any religious value, constitute "merit", in whatever way that may be understood'.[48]

Bouyer traces three stages in the development of Protestantism. First came the rediscovery of a neglected aspect of Catholic truth. This, in itself positive and good, rouses opposition from those who cannot or will not see it, which drove the Reformers to proclaim it with a protective exclusiveness that over-defines and distorts. The second stage is thus reached, whereby a new orthodoxy shores up the particular Catholic truth with a negative casing that invites a corresponding reaction on the other side. A Protestant scholasticism soon faces a Counter-Reformation. Positions are locked in controversy. The Protestant scholasticism then follows the path of its medieval Catholic predecessor: ever closer definition, polarization into its own rival 'schools', harsh exaggeration. The third stage occurs when people tire of the rigid orthodoxy. Now and then the real dynamic bursts out in revival, but the merely nominal adherents drift into indifferentism. Moral earnestness replaces religious fervour until the secular Protestants return full cycle to a position of salvation by moral excellence indistinguishable in principle from that against which the Reformers first reacted.

Indifference in matters of theological doctrine fits easily into the general outlook of the late twentieth century. The nineteen-fifties were the last decade when it was easy for many people to accept historic Christianity. The sixties saw an upheaval when the implications of scientific advance, especially the bio-chemical possibilities for modifying human existence, became widely known. The existence of a supernatural or spiritual realm was questioned, not least among theologians. Many felt obliged to limit theological statement to that which could be verified in human behaviour.

The nineteen-seventies saw development and reaction. The sixties were worried over speaking about God. Interest in the seventies centred on whether you can speak about Jesus as the Son of God in a manner that marks him as different in kind from other human beings. It was a natural development, for if you are not happy to say much about God, you will not be at home with notions of Christ that make him start with God, beyond humanity. The doctrine of Christ's pre-existence and the Fourth Gospel are suspect in many learned quarters, though the popularity of the latter with ordinary believers has not declined. The trend has, if anything, intensified as the nineteen-seventies pass into the eighties.

The 'general outlook of the late twentieth century' could be said to include a secular orthodoxy to which many of those who promote the tone of public opinion subscribe. Theologians have welcomed its humanitarian elements, which they rightly conclude to be evidence of Christian influence. Taken as a whole, however, they have been far too complacent in accepting the canons of the new orthodoxy. But some voices have been raised in protest. A group of theologians, for example, met in America, where acceptance of secular theology has been widespread, in 1974. They included members of many different Churches, among them Orthodox, Roman Catholic, and Anglican, and met at Hartford, Connecticut under the chairmanship of Pastor Richard J. Neuhaus and the sociologist Peter L. Berger. Their main concern was the loss of a sense of the transcendent, which they felt to be seriously undermining Christian faith and practice. Painstaking inquiry into the cause of this loss led them to isolate thirteen 'themes' prominent in secular thought and largely assumed by theologians. 'Many are superficially attractive,' they wrote, 'but upon closer examination we find these themes false and debilitating to the Church's life and work.'[49]

The thirteen themes make an admirable form of self-examination for a theologian in his own devotions. I set them out here as heads for reflection; the full text may be found in Fr Avery Dulles's book *The Resilient Church*.[50]

Modern thought is superior to all past forms of understanding reality, and is therefore normative for Christian faith and life.

Religious statements are totally independent of reasonable discourse.

Religious language refers to human experience and nothing else, God being humanity's noblest creation.

Jesus can only be understood in terms of contemporary models of humanity.

All religions are equally valid; the choice among them is not a matter of conviction about truth but only of personal preference or lifestyle.

To realize one's potential and to be true to oneself is the whole meaning of salvation.

Since what is human is good, evil can adequately be understood as failure to realize potential.

The sole purpose of worship is to promote individual self-realization and human community.

Institutions and historical traditions are oppressive and inimical to our being truly human; liberation from them is required for authentic existence and authentic religion.

The world must set the agenda for the Church. Social, political, and economic programs to improve the quality of life are ultimately normative for the Church's mission in the world.

An emphasis on God's transcendence is at least a hindrance to, and perhaps incompatible with, Christian social concern and action.

The struggle for a better humanity will bring about the Kingdom of God.

The question of hope beyond death is irrelevant or at best marginal to the Christian understanding of human fulfillment.

The Hartford Appeal is negative. It fires a shot across the bows of those who sail the Church too close to the prevailing winds of today's opinions. For that alone we should be grateful. It sets a question mark beside most of the attitudes which undermine the function of dogmatic theology. It does not suggest any particular orthodoxy, nor is it fundamentalist in urging a return to the letter of any confession of faith. For that, too, we may be grateful. Positively, it clears the ground for a more favourable estimate for religious faith authoritatively declared, and for that we may be the most grateful of all.

The absence of the note of authority conspicuously weakens the Christian mission today. The psychological lesson that authoritarian pronouncements often disguise weakness or insecurity has contributed to a devaluation of all authority. We should distinguish between authoritarian and authoritative. An authoritarian approach discourages questioning and seeks to impose obedience: 'You don't do that, because Daddy says you mustn't', to put it in nursery terms. An authoritative approach, on the other hand, commends itself from its own position of strength, thus eliciting obedience: 'Don't do that, because if you do, you'll burn your hand.' The first is rightly rejected for being out of place in religion, and indeed in most other things. The second is wrongly confused with it. True religion is necessarily authoritative, for its intrinsic authenticity issues a summons to obey. Sometimes, of course, it is that very notion of obedience that is considered undesirable. If so, one can only ask why? – and perhaps draw on psychology for an answer.

Does the Church rightly include any centre or organ which requires obedience of the faithful? If the answer of this book is Yes, it is given with the proviso that the authority implied is not that of human greatness. Jesus came among his contemporaries as one who served, and the Gospels agree that when it was a question of disciples carrying on his leadership, their authority was to be that of a servant. Christian authority is there for the sake of those who obey; ministers of whatever sort are those who serve – ironically, perhaps, the word itself means that. Among the proudest of the pope's titles is *servus servorum Dei*, slave of the slaves of God. Pope John was the first to fire millions outside as well as within the Roman Catholic Church with a vision of what that might mean. Pope Paul VI, of a less ebullient character, secured the vision by giving himself to a degree of personal suffering which recalled his apostolic namesake. In his brief pontificate of thirty-three days, Pope John Paul I symbolized his declared intention to be above all a serving pope by his refusal to be crowned. Pope John Paul II, formed in the sterner mould of a church behind the Iron Curtain, seems set to extend the trail his predecessors blazed into the end of this century. No doubt the screw needs a good few more turns before the true authority of service is understood throughout all the structures of ecclesiastical power. But Christian service, it must be stressed, is not abject. Servants are called to be friends of the Lord whose service is perfect freedom. There is nothing servile in living by truly authoritative religion; humility is not humiliating. Properly authoritative religious teaching is indeed to be welcomed, for it delivers us from the restriction of supposing our own experience and judgement to be the best that could possibly be.

5
REVELATION

The Catholic faith is an objective and permanent body of teaching. It is authoritative because it preserves what God has made known; that it has proved and proves convincing is secondary. Christianity is not in the end the human search for God, but God's self-disclosure within mankind, which takes up and sets in order the confused yearnings of the human spirit. The theological problem is whether the divine message has been clearly received.

The doctrine of revelation, to give this disclosure its technical name, is widely disliked today. The themes of modernity combine to reject the possibility that God discloses his ways in such a fashion as to command obedience. So far as theology is in bondage to modernity, it will avoid connecting too closely the historic deposit of faith with a revelation for today. Only in the authoritative teaching of conservative Protestantism or in churches which set great store by tradition is there an emphasis on revealed truth.

The dislike is recent. The years between the two World Wars saw a new emphasis on God's revelation as Christians on the Continent, disillusioned by the failure of Liberal Protestantism to speak a word of prophecy to the crumbling world of European ascendancy, turned again to their Bibles. Karl Barth, of course, is the most famous name. Anglican theology, always more restrained than its Lutheran or Calvinist counterpart, followed in moderation the same course. During the nineteen-fifties, the new interest in the theology contained in the Bible itself combined with a deeper awareness of what it meant to 'be the Church' to restore an authoritative note to Anglican teaching generally. But it burst like a bubble when touched by 'sixties' secularism. Since then, all except in the several conservative pockets has been tentative, basing itself little on the norms of Bible or Church, but taking its cue from each passing situation.

'Had Cleopatra's nose been shorter, the whole history of the world would have been different.' But would it? Pascal's great might-have-been cuts little ice today, for the notion that enormous consequences hang on tiny accidents is alien. That is the clue to the unpopularity of revelation in its traditional form. For revelation is at heart Jesus Christ. The whole inconceivable immensity of God was focused in the life and death of one man in an obscure part of the long-dead Roman Empire. It is sometimes called 'the scandal of particularity', and it certainly makes many of our contemporaries stumble.

But not our contemporaries only. The present age prides itself on being different from its predecessors. In this matter at least its pride is ill-founded. The great majority of Jesus's own contemporaries, even his acquaintances, failed to recognize him for what he was. The authorities in Church and state clearly had not time for the claims of his followers. The early history of the Church shows abundant traces in its scanty literature of cultured despisers. The true worth of Jesus has never been self-evident. St Paul underlined the fact that among the first believers

> not many were powerful, not many were of noble birth; but God chose what is foolish in the world to shame the wise, God chose what is weak in the world to shame the strong, God chose what is low and

despised in the world, even things that are not, to bring to nothing things that are.[51]

He spells out the purpose of such paradoxical choice: 'So that no human being might boast in the presence of God.' The first two chapters of 1 Corinthians set out a first generation understanding of God's revelation through Jesus. It is not made to human excellence, whether of intellect, morals, or piety. That is quite clear.

It is equally clear that those who were chosen, even the least likely of them, have recognized the truth unerringly. That is because they were enabled by the Holy Spirit. The great ones of the world saw and misunderstood, and

> crucified the Lord of glory. But, as it is written,
> 'What no eye has seen, nor ear heard,
> nor the heart of man conceived,
> what God has prepared for those who love him,'
> God has revealed to us through the Spirit.[52]

This Spirit is God's agent, or God in action (we should not expect to find in St Paul the trinitarian precision achieved after two or three centuries of Christian experience).

> For the Spirit searches everything, even the depths of God. For what person knows a man's thoughts except the spirit of the man which is in him? So also no one comprehends the thoughts of God except the Spirit of God.[53]

The implication of that last sentence would be breathtaking in its arrogance were the subject religious awareness instead of divine revelation.

To have been admitted to the thoughts of God was an experience which Paul must have found he shared with Peter when he visited him in Jerusalem. Paul's background was that of rabbi whose rigorous training placed him in a class quite above that of an unlettered Galilean fisherman; the shock of discovering that such distinctions vanish when God reveals himself may be reflected in the first passage quoted above.

> 'But who do you say that I am?' Simon Peter replied, 'You are the Christ, the Son of the living God.' And Jesus answered him, 'Blessed

are you, Simon Bar-Jona! For flesh and blood has not revealed this
to you, but my Father who is in heaven.'[54]

Christianity is, at its deepest points, revelation. At its heart lie
events and claims which are, from the unaided human standpoint, ridiculous. They may be known as truth only in that
mysterious exchange where Spirit meets spirit and a human
being is admitted into the counsels of God. That was what
happened when the Church was founded, and the revelation
made to the apostles was deposited in a community where it
could be preserved to be the means of enlightening the
generations to come.

Catholic teaching has always insisted on the mystery of revelation. It is often exasperating, but it should not be surprising
when the leaders of human opinion fail to understand matters
that to a Christian are as plain as a pikestaff. Even after the
revelation there is still mystery in the relation between belief,
unbelief, and ignorance. In many cases unbelief is so deeply
conditioned that the person trapped in it is 'invincibly ignorant'
so that no personal guilt attaches to him or her. Yet in itself, ignorance is inexcusable. There are those who use it as a shield,
who see and will not admit that they see;

> For what can be known about God is plain to them, because God has
> shown it to them. Ever since the creation of the world his invisible
> nature, namely, his eternal power and deity, has been clearly
> perceived in the things that have been made. So they are without
> excuse. . . .[55]

St Paul goes on to explain to the Romans how that inexcusable
atheism is often maintained by vested interests. The atheist
could not afford to admit the existence of God.

Common sense, common experience, suggest the existence of
God. Sophisticates ancient and modern find difficulties, but
simple people are not natural atheists. Thus again St Paul, according to the author of Acts, this time to the pagans of Lystra:

> We also are men, of like nature with you, and bring you good news,
> that you should turn from these vain things to a living God who
> made the heaven and the earth and the sea and all that is in them. In
> past generations he allowed all the nations to walk in their own

ways; yet he did not leave himself without witness, for he did good and gave you from heaven rains and fruitful seasons, satisfying your hearts with food and gladness.[56]

With the cultured despisers on the Areopagus in Athens, St Paul took a line basically similar, though tricked out to keep the attention of that difficult audience. God was to be perceived behind the phenomena that made life possible. Taking his cue from a shrine dedicated to 'an unknown God', the apostle declared:

> What therefore you worship as unknown, this I proclaim to you. The God who made the world and everything in it, being Lord of heaven and earth, does not live in shrines made by man, nor is he served by human hands, as though he needed anything, since he himself gives to all men life and breath and everything. And he made from one every nation of men to live on all the face of the earth, having determined allotted periods and the boundaries of their habitation, that they should seek God, in the hope that they might feel after him and find him. Yet he is not far from each one of us. . . .[57]

and he backs it with quotations from two Greek authors. Thus far, we may suppose, Paul carried his audience. Then he came to the mystery.

> Being then God's offspring, we ought not to think that the Deity is like gold, or silver, or stone, a representation by the art and imagination of man. The times of ignorance God overlooked, but now he commands all men everywhere to repent, because he has fixed a day on which he will judge the world in righteousness by a man who he has appointed, and of this he has given assurance to all men by raising him from the dead.[58]

At that point some laughed, others wanted to hear more, a few believed. That was where natural reason failed and conviction could come only by the Spirit.

Belief in revelation of truth beyond the grasp of unaided reason has marked all forms of Christianity except those aberrations which have tried to confine it within the limits of common sense. But there has been controversy over whether the revelation, properly speaking, was confined to the apostolic generation. 'Sir, the pretending to extraordinary revelations and gifts of the Holy Ghost is a horrid thing, a very horrid thing,' said Bishop Butler to John Wesley. The problem was not new. The main lines of Catholic orthodoxy were hammered out in the century that followed the New Testament largely to distinguish the authentic revelation from a growing body of additions or alternatives. The problem of whether God might extend his revelation after the passing of the apostolic generation was settled by the assumption that anything new had to establish itself as an implication of what had been revealed in the age of the apostles. Hence the importance attached to apostolic authorship of any piece of Christian writing which claimed to belong to the canon of Scripture.

Revealed truth, however, was not frozen in the actual words of Scripture. That was made clear after the Council of Nicaea in 325. The Arians, confining themselves to the words of Scripture, had insisted that Jesus the Christ was altogether different from God, for 'there was a time when he was not'. 'Proofs' from Scripture could be readily cited in support. Athanasius bishop of Alexandria insisted that nevertheless Christ must be understood as being 'of one substance' with the Father. The Arians and their fellow-travellers, including for one agonized moment the bishop of Rome himself, cried innovator. Athanasius persisted even in exile and the Christian consensus, including the same Liberius of Rome who, like Peter before him, had yielded to pressure, came to side with him. *Homoousios*, the Greek word at issue, was not a New Testament word, but it conveyed what the New Testament really meant. One hundred years later, a similar dispute ended by legitimating the non-biblical *theotokos*, mother of God, as describing suitably Jesus's mother.

For a thousand years the matter was little discussed. A major battle had in fact been won. It can best be appreciated by reference to the history of Islam, the religion which arose in Arabia and spread round the Mediterranean to become Christianity's most dangerous rival. Islam, like Christianity, is a religion of revelation, and that revelation centred on a holy book. But the connection with the letter of the book was much tighter. The Qurân might not be translated from the Arabic. More was at stake than respect for a sacred language, for language enshrines culture within distinctive concepts: standard ways of looking at things. Christianity was equipped to be a faith for the whole human race just because its concepts could find their level in different speech and within different cultures from that in which they started. By admitting the *homoousios*, the Church decisively accepted the cultural translation of revealed truth.

At the Reformation, the issue proved among the most divisive. In one form or another all the Reformers accused the medieval Church of innovation, and challenged its current teaching in the name of the original faith, discernible from the Bible. The matter turned on the relative authority of Scripture and tradition; Catholic and Protestant agreed in deploring a third view, that behind both Scripture and tradition stood the authority of religious awareness quickened by direct action of the Spirit. The third view in the sixteenth century marked off small sects that were persecuted as much for political as for religious subversion. It persisted as an interior challenge among Protestants and Catholics alike, and a secular form of it triumphed at the Enlightenment of the eighteenth century. Its influence may be traced in many of today's secular themes.

The issue of Bible versus tradition hardened into the principal theological contention between Catholic and Protestant. Recent studies suggest that even at the time the struggle was more ideological than theological, for the best representatives of both sides stood closer together than they realized. George H. Tavard in *Holy Writ or Holy Church* showed how the heat of battle between the English controversialists John Jewel and Thomas Harding kept both men from seeing how narrow was the gap that separated them.[59] And when the Council of Trent formulated the doctrine to include the phrase 'this truth and discipline is contained in written books and in unwritten traditions which, received by the apostles from the mouth of Christ himself, or from the apostles themselves, the Holy Ghost dictating, have come down transmitted as it were hand to hand',[60] it did not commit the Church to the view that revelation was partly in the Bible, partly in unwritten traditions, as controversialists too easily supposed. And Louis Bouyer insists that 'the supreme authority of Scripture, taken in its positive sense, as gradually drawn out and systematized by the Protestants themselves, far from setting the Church and Protestantism in opposition, should be the best possible warrant for their returning to unity and understanding.'[61]

Recent developments in biblical study, to which increasingly Catholic scholars have contributed alongside their Protestant colleagues, add realism to Bouyer's hopeful judgement. The formation of the New Testament itself took place in a context of tradition. It is no longer possible to read the Gospels as if they were chapter one to the Epistles' chapter two; the Gospel record of Jesus does not convey an impression of him except through the later experience of his disciples. Any doctrine of inspiration must take into account the evidence within the New Testament writings of how they came to be written. The New Testament conveys the Word of God in the words of men and is none the less inspired for that. The New Testament in all its variety was put together within the life of the Church, and any biblicism which considers the New Testament as a text in isolation from its living context is simply unhistorical. It is now clear, on grounds of rigorous historical criticism, that the Council of Trent was wiser than was once thought in refusing to isolate Scripture from tradition. The relationship between the two is complex. But, as Vatican II made clear, 'Sacred Tradition and sacred Scripture, then, are bound closely together, and communicate with one another. For both of them, flowing out from the same divine well-spring, come together in some fashion to form one thing, and move towards the same goal.'[62]

Vatican II's emphasis on the God who reveals opened new possibilities of outflanking entrenched positions based on the revelation. 'Sacred Scripture is the speech of God as it is put down in writing under the breath of the Holy Spirit. And Tradition transmits in its entirety the Word of God which has been entrusted to the apostles by Christ the Lord and the Holy Spirit.'[63] Tradition and Scripture thus 'make up a single sacred deposit of the Word of God, which is entrusted to the Church.'[64] This account removes the embarrassment caused by the isolation of Scripture whereby it becomes a holy book which descended one and complete from the hand of the Lord. Justice may now be done to the Bible's internal evidence of diversity in approach as well as in date, and also to the process by which those particular books were deemed to be canonical. It sets the several books in their own historical context, thus securing to them the authority of human integrity. It raises also other problems.

Protestant theologians have argued at length over whether the revelation is personal or propositional; that is, whether the truth lies in the actual form of words used, or in the relationship between God and man, or among humankind, which the words relate to. Today's controversy is a relic of the nineteenth-century phase of the battle between science and religion, when champions of biblical authority invested the words of Scripture with an infallibility that had not hitherto been so precisely attributed to them. The Word of God was equated with the words of Scripture; it was possible to speak of 'the Word enscriptured' as correlative to 'the Word incarnate'. A particular form of the argument turned upon the Lord's own use of Old Testament Scripture. The view forms part of an integrated theological system, a form of Calvinism associated particularly with the Free University of Amsterdam, with the Fundamentalists (properly so called) in the USA, and with the Anglican Conservative Evangelicals.[65] A defensive and often pietistically anti-intellectual movement until about 1950, it can now claim an impressive record of theological scholarship. The propositional nature of revelation remains a central tenet, and it is this particularly that marks it off from the revival of authoritative Protestantism associated with Karl Barth.

Protestant Christianity is divided by this issue, it seems beyond hope; for there is no middle ground. Perhaps it will only be united when the doctrine of revelation is as it were linked at both ends: to the One who reveals; and to an agent on the human side who can interpret authoritatively that which is revealed. Certainly some of the guidelines that have come from Rome since Vatican II indicate a framework able to contain both freedom of critical scholarship and respect for the divine authority of Scripture. In 1964, for example, the Pontifical Biblical Commission issued an Instruction which understood the Gospels to have reached their final form through three stages.[66] The first, the actual teaching of Jesus, was not directly recorded. The second was the preaching of the apostles which resulted in the founding of local churches whose members needed instruction according to a fixed tradition. It was to fill that need that the Gospels were written. Friction between scholars in a university setting and the Doctrinal Congregation at Rome continue, but the Congregation's Declaration of 1973, *Mysterium Ecclesiae*, while checking certain views which it believed to infringe Catholic orthodoxy, reinforced the need to take seriously the historical conditioning of dogma. That which is revealed with divine authority is revealed in human words. The Declaration repeated Pope John's fine words at the opening of the Council:

> This certain and unchangeable doctrine, to which faithful obedience is due, has to be explored and presented in a way that is demanded by our times. The deposit of faith, which consists of the truths contained in sacred doctrine, is one thing, the manner of presentation, always however with the same meaning and signification, is something else.[67]

The Congregation reminded its readers of similar words spoken by Pope Paul:

> Nowadays a serious effort is required of us to ensure that the teaching of the faith should keep the fullness of its meaning and force, while expressing itself in a form which allows itself to reach the spirit and heart of the people to whom it is addressed.[68]

6
MAGISTERIUM

It is not fashionable to praise the magisterium of the Catholic Church. The formal, official teaching office is so often presented as an obstacle to progress that it has become a bogey, not least to Roman Catholics. Yet the argument of the last section suggested that something like a magisterium – 'an agent on the human side who can interpret authoritatively that which is revealed' – is needed. The Eastern Orthodox churches after all have their tradition, that self-contained coherence of belief, worship, and practice which fascinates and bewilders those outside, for it is at once elusive and effective. Most Protestant bodies have a confession of faith included as it were among their title deeds, and in most there are different attitudes towards that confession. The Anglican Communion is in a peculiar position in that its historic confession, the Thirty-Nine Articles of the Church of England, is not the doctrinal standard in defence of which it began its independent life, but a statement adopted some years later to distinguish it from other forms of Christianity. Its original claim against Rome was that it represented the Catholic faith more faithfully than Rome did, so that its standards were the common creeds of Christendom. But it would be hard to find any simple statement of its teaching authority to which all Anglicans would agree.[69]

Magisterium as a concept repels because it is Latin, and because it is legal; it is thus alien to English ways. 'Teaching office' is worse, for it cannot avoid suggesting bureaucracy. It also sounds stuffy. We will persevere with magisterium, for it is so alien that our definition will not be weighted down by wrong associations. Here is a classic modern statement:

> Sacred Tradition and sacred Scripture make up a single sacred deposit of the Word of God, which is entrusted to the Church. . . .
>
> But the task of giving an authentic interpretation of the Word of God, whether in its written form or in the form of tradition, has been entrusted to the living teaching office of the Church alone. Its authority in this matter is exercised in the name of Jesus Christ. Yet this magisterium is not superior to the Word of God, but is its servant. It teaches only what has been handed on to it. At the divine command and with the help of the Holy Spirit, it listens to this devotedly, guards it with dedication, and expounds it faithfully. All that it proposes for belief is drawn from this single deposit of faith.[70]

The magisterium is thus correlative to tradition and Scripture. Yet it is to the 'living teaching office' (*vivo ecclesiae magisterio*) that the authentic interpretation is committed. This is no abstraction but a collection of people. What people? It may be most variously described: pope, bishops, the community of the faithful. The Church's 'ordinary' magisterium is its everyday teaching on faith and morals, faithfully relayed. The local bishop applying the Church's teaching to an immediate situation is exercising the magisterium. So is the mother who, basing herself on the Church's teaching, teaches her child to pray. All such instances of the Church's living faith relate to the magisterium, however far they may be from the centre of hierarchy. In their fidelity they draw on the same well of spiritual authority. But the authority thus diffused has its centre, the well from which the water springs pure, the source of certainty in cases of doubt.

That, declared Vatican II, is located in the college of bishops, with the pope at their head.

> Just as, in accordance with the Lord's decree, St Peter and the rest of the apostles constitute a unique apostolic college, so in like fashion the Roman Pontiff, Peter's successor, and the bishops, the successors of the apostles, are related with and united to one another.[71]

Vatican II's emphasis on bishops is new, for Vatican I had tended to exalt the pope's authority by depressing theirs, a trend increased in curial practice. The doctrine, unlike the emphasis, is not new. The principle of collegiality does not lessen the pope's authority; it gives it the proper context.

But how, in practice, is the college of bishops able to express itself? The only time when they all meet is in General Council, of which there have been three since the mid-sixteenth century. The Synod of Bishops has been devised to express corporate opinion. It will be most effective when backed by regular meetings on a provincial or national basis. In addition, diocesan bishops are now represented on the various organs of the Curia. And modern communications make it far easier than it used to be to sound out general opinion. But many Catholics believe that all this is far too small to make much difference. The Curia is a highly specialized organization, a complex bureaucracy and, as any such body will, it has developed its own means of protection from disturbing change. Visiting bishops entering its deliberations will easily be manoeuvred into positions of maximum honour and minimum power, and there will be ways of dealing with those who do not conform. An observer of the Vatican scene has contrasted Pope Paul's increasing use of the Secretary of State (or his Sostituto) as his link with all curial departments with Pope John Paul II's restoration of a large measure of independence to the Congregation for the Doctrine of the Faith.[72] Neither development, he believes, encourages true collegiality.

Time may well answer these criticisms. The Council ended in 1965. Decisions of theological principle had been taken, among them the collegiality of bishops with the pope at their head, which in the end cannot avoid affecting even the most entrenched central administration. But it will take time. Indeed, it could hardly be otherwise, for the Church's work must go on without interruption in its everyday routines.

A more serious criticism of the magisterium since Vatican II questions the appropriateness of expecting the bishops collectively to be the arbiters of proper teaching. The complexity of modern knowledge is such that often responsible judgement can be made only after listening to many specialisms at a level where few are equipped to understand. It is absurd to suppose that bishops, whose specialism presumably lies in the more pastoral skills of theology, are thus equipped. Faced with the challenge of the unfamiliar, they will opt for the old ways. But why should this authority reside in the episcopate? Ministry in the early Church was exercised first by apostles, 'second prophets, third teachers, then workers of miracles, then healers, helpers, administrators, speakers in various kinds of tongues'.[73] That list suggests a measure of hierarchical grading, though the allowance must be made for the situation at Corinth where the 'speakers in various kinds of tongues' had got thoroughly out of hand. In the letter to the Ephesians (in the opinion of many, not directly St Paul's) another list declares that Christ's gifts to his Church were 'that some should be apostles, some prophets, some evangelists, some pastors and teachers'.[74] The same epistle describes the Church in the metaphor of a temple 'built upon the foundation of the apostles and prophets, Christ Jesus himself being the chief cornerstone'.[75] It says also that the great truth of the unity of Jew and Gentile in Christ 'has now been revealed to his holy apostles and prophets by the Spirit'.[76] Why should the authority of all these separate aspects of ministry now be concentrated in the one magisterium so that bishops-in-college with the pope at their head are expected to act for apostles, prophets, and teachers? Surely the last category at least – teachers – is best represented in the modern Church by theologians and scholars of other disciplines.

Both criticisms turn on the place of the expert, and the relation of the theologian to the Church's teaching office. Recent arguments on this subject tend to take as an example the issue of artificial birth prevention and the encyclical *Humanae Vitae*, so we will consider it in that connection, in the next chapter.

Local churches in New Testament times varied considerably in their internal organization. By the end of the second century, a monarchical (i.e., single ruler) episcopate had become the standard. The factors behind this change are not all known, but one of them was evidently the need to protect congregations from the revelations of self-styled prophets, whose teachings may have been more exciting than the basic tradition of which the bishop was the appointed guardian. The Jesuit theologian Karl Rahner has pointed out the two elements in that apostolic tradition of teaching for which the earliest Fathers looked to bishops whose successions went back to the apostles.

> One is the material element, the doctrine of the apostles about the Christ-event (in the broadest sense) which is handed on and given the expression corresponding to the needs of the times. The other is the formal or active element, the claim of the bishops to demand faith as they testify in the name of Christ and with the assistance of the Holy Spirit.[77]

The first element is that succession of doctrine on which conservative Protestants as much as Catholics would insist. The second element relates the succession of doctrine to the historical structure of the continuing community, which marks a difference between Catholic and Protestant. The Protestant believes that the structure belongs to an altogether lower level of importance than the doctrine. The Roman Catholic (Eastern Orthodox and many Anglo–Catholics would agree) holds the two to be inseparable.

The magisterium of the Church derives its importance from the finality of Christ. Rahner, for whom the magisterium is, of course, infallible, shows that with Christ something unprecedented entered the human scene. This was no mere messenger of God, but the Son: no mere teacher of righteousness but the one who has brought in the new age. For the totality of Christ, Rahner uses the phrase 'Christ-event', and he calls the total effect of that event its 'eschatological triumph'. This is God's last word to man, the ultimate destiny reserved for mankind in the divine purpose; the end in the sense of completeness, fulfilment. Part of what gives to the Christ-event its finality is 'the word which it testifies to itself. It can only remain eschatologically present and triumphant in the world if it does not falter and fail in the word of self-attestation'.[78] Its consequence is a new religious certainty.

The Catholic understanding of magisterium must therefore be considered in relation to Christ's continuing presence in the world, a triumphant presence. Such a conception is not absent from Protestant theology, though it is often expressed through an image which excludes or at least masks the note of triumph. Protestants, accustomed to discern truth with difficulty from within the brokenness of separate denominations, look especially to the suffering Christ humiliated in the dehumanized structures of man's inhumanity to man. The Protestant reacts negatively to the notion of triumph in the Church and so to the certainties of Catholic teaching. But does not the Christian gospel declare that Christ has triumphed over suffering, in and through humiliation? Ironically, Catholic teaching with its triumphant note of certainty suggests the Protestant preference for the open cross to the crucifix. It is in harmony with the Protestant insistence that the Church lives by the risen Christ, not the dead Christ of Calvary.

'This word of testimony, by which the Christ-event becomes historically present to all ages, is uttered primarily by the whole community of Christian believers, by the Church as such and as a whole.'[79] The key thought which Rahner develops is that of the actual presence of Christ, not the mere honouring of his memory. Magisterium is a matter of God's present activity before it is a human response. But the Church that makes the response 'is something more than the mere sum of individual believers, totted up as it were from below. It is not just a meta-historical fellowship, but a historically-structured society with a

confession of faith and a doctrinal authority.'[80] Only in that
context can the Church dare to claim an authority which in any
simply human setting would be both arrogant and ridiculous.
The magisterium in its certainty gives effect to God's will that the
saving truth of Christ should be present in the world until the
end of time. It is therefore misleading to consider the
magisterium only in terms of defining doctrine. That is indeed
one function, but it is only one in a scale which 'ranges', as
Rahner puts it, 'from the seemingly merely doctrinal pro-
clamations of magisterium, and the directives which define a
Christian task in a given situation of the Church and the individual, to the word which is the "form" in the sacrament and
makes the grace of God historically present and effective *ex opere
operato*'.[81]

The magisterium of the Church is no less than the authority of
Christ present in the world. But it is experienced through the
limitations of history; and here we meet the theme of the continued humiliation of the Triumphant. It is evident therefore
that accepting the magisterium does not mean accepting the
human arrangements through which the voice of the
magisterium is heard. Such acceptance is compatible with constructive criticism and reforming zeal, and indeed obedience
may even demand them both. Loyalty may well be critical as well
as constant; a matter to which we return in the next chapter.

The magisterium, it should be said, is not necessarily a drag
on the Church. Its conservative tendency infuriates progressives,
but it saves the Church from being blown one way and another
by successive winds of enthusiasm. It stabilizes the Church.
More positively, the existence of a strong corporate authority
bears important witness to an aspect of truth. 'Truth', in Karl
Rahner's words, 'of its very nature has to do with fellowship,
society, and institutions.' It is not to be found in abstract
doctrine but in doctrine by which the institution lives. The true
faith is not my own but the Church's, in which I have a share.
The authority of the Church to which the individual commits
himself may well have a wider appeal than that of a personally
held conviction which the individual accepts or rejects without
the implication of belonging to a fellowship. He will indeed
commit himself beyond the limits of his understanding, in

places perhaps against his own inclinations. The truth is greater than any individual's grasp of it, and he will treat it more seriously when he allows himself 'to be corrected by the truth which is not *a priori* his own but comes to him as that of a socially instituted fellowship'.[82]

Or, as G. K. Chesterton put it two generations ago, 'We do not really want a religion that is right where we are right. What we want is a religion that is right where we are wrong.'[83] For the real triumph of the Catholic faith 'is not in merely being right where we are right, as in being cheerful or hopeful or human. It is in having been right where we are wrong, and in the fact coming back upon us afterwards like a boomerang.'[84]

7

INFALLIBILITY

The life of the Church is the life of Christ who dwells at its heart, according to his promise: 'Where two or three are gathered in my name, there am I in the midst of them.' St Matthew records those words in a passage which deals with church discipline.[85] They do not refer to a flight of mystical experience, but to the hard grind of community living where love must work through structures which cannot exclude the juridical. It is in that perspective that we should understand the Catholic claim to infallibility in matters of faith and morals. However deeply particular formulations of teaching may be conditioned by the language and thought forms of their age, the word of God may be discerned in them. Protestants often assume that grounding infallibility upon the indwelling Christ is an attempt to clothe with divine authority teachings which are essentially human. But Catholics hold that infallibility begins with God, who alone is absolutely infallible. Any infallibility in the Church is derived from God's. In the words of *Mysterium Ecclesiae,*

> God, who is absolutely infallible, thus designed to bestow upon his new people, which is the Church, a certain shared infallibility, which is restricted to matters of faith and morals, which is present when the whole People of God unhesitatingly holds a point of doctrine pertaining to these matters, and finally which always depends upon the

wise providence and anointing grace of the Holy Spirit, who leads the Church into all truth until the glorious coming of her Lord.[86]

The Declaration which includes that statement was issued in 1973 to check recent Catholic studies that had played down the element of infallibility in Church teaching, notably, it is believed, some of Dr Hans Küng's work. Even so, many Protestants must be surprised at the moderation of those claims. Compared with Conservative Evangelical beliefs about the infallibility of Scripture, the area of church teaching for which infallibility is claimed is small indeed. Nor is this moderation a result of Vatican II. 'With regard to the doctrinal teaching of the Church it must be well noted that not all the assertions of the Teaching Authority of the Church on questions of faith and morals are infallible and consequently irrevocable,' wrote Dr Ott.[87] The pre-Vatican II 'manualist' continues: Only those are infallible which emanate from General Councils representing the whole episcopate, and the papal decisions *ex cathedra*.' The pope's ordinary teaching activities are not protected by infallibility, nor are the decisions of Roman Congregations. Protestant and Catholic alike often assume that much more is covered than actually is the case.

But what exactly is infallibility? Dr Ott gives a convenient summary:

Infallibility is the impossibility of falling into error. One may distinguish an active and a passive infallibility. The former belongs to the pastors of the Church in the exercise of their teaching office . . . , the latter to the faithful as a whole in its assent to the message of faith. . . . Active and passive are related as cause and effect. . . .[88]

Discussion must therefore centre on the active form. It will be well immediately to dispose of two misunderstandings. Infallibility does not mean sinlessness. It has nothing to do with the moral worth of any person or group which is held to exercise it. Nor is it the product of outstanding intelligence, sensitivity, holiness, or other human excellence, though no doubt it can work through these qualities. The infallibility of the Church does not derive from the quality of its human leadership, for it is a communication of God's infallibility.

Infallibility is exercised through the Church's magisterium, so there is little to add to what was said in the previous chapter about where it is located. It is found to be basically in the Church as the community gathered around the Lord. Specific definitions of truth are needed only when disagreement cannot be settled by the ordinary means of forming a consensus, and it will be made through whatever organ is held at the time to be the proper authority. History shows a growing precision. In the early days the matter was little discussed, but a touchstone of truth was implied in the appeal made to the rule of faith or the deposit of truth when some teaching was in doubt. The authority of the General Councils which defined the Trinity and the incarnation was assumed without question and such decisions once accepted were binding. The modern debate began when the Conciliar Movement challenged the authority of a pope all too evidently swayed by secular interests. That issue was finally settled in the pope's favour at the First Vatican Council. The Second Vatican Council came after the Church had had nearly a century's experience of ruling through moral rather than political muscle and was relaxed enough to tease out the nuances of Vatican I's basic decision. That process is still far from complete.

The infallibility of the Church is thus correlative to its magisterium. There is the same surface contradiction between the mode of the servant and the triumphant mode. The Church exists to serve the world and yet it makes dogmatic pronouncements to which it expects the world to listen. Perhaps the most glaring example of recent years was the dogmatic definition of the Blessed Virgin's assumption, for which infallibility was specifically claimed. It seemed to many in 1950 that to declare as an article of belief needful for salvation that 'the Immaculate Mother of God, the ever Virgin Mary, when the course of her earthly life was run, was assumed in body and in soul to heavenly glory'[89] was an act of reckless triumphalism. The description of the Lord's mother in the definition and the way of speaking about heaven showed utter contempt for modern views that look to this world for human vindication. To declare a belief that could show so little grounding in Scripture or even in explicit tradition to be an essential part of the Catholic faith flew in the face of that Christian consensus which the Ecumenical Movement was laboriously trying to create.

A quarter of a century later, the situation has quite changed. Rome has shed much of its outward triumphalism, has shouldered more evidently the burdens of a servant. But the dogma of 1950 stands firm. The Vatican II Constitution on the Church changed the dogma of Mary's assumption from a gesture of contempt for modern man to 'a sign of hope and comfort for the pilgrim people of God'.[90] Catholic teaching about Mary was now integrated into the main body of belief, so that what had seemed increasingly aberrant was now shown to be a healthy development of the basic faith. Pope Paul's great Apostolic Exhortation *Marialis Cultus*[91] went on to emphasize the social as well as the theological importance of the Marian theme, helping to bring it to the centre of ecumenical concern. But it is the recent tendency to attack the traditional understanding of Jesus as the incarnate Son of God which has shown how important and how timely was the dogma proclaimed in 1950. If Jesus was not the incarnate Son of God, no one would believe such things about his mother. Catholics who are committed to defined Marian teaching will not easily forsake their belief in her Son. The theological extravagance of 1950 now has a key role in defending historic Christianity's inmost beliefs.

The world of today, theologically as in other ways, is very different from the one which first heard St Matthew's Gospel, with its promise that Jesus would be with his people when they gathered formally to decide some contentious matter. But, the Catholic Christian claims, the change is one of outward circumstances only. The inner dynamics remain constant.

The conviction that the Lord may be experienced as present in his Church underlies the Catholic appeal to infallibility. It can be explored by approaching those New Testament passages which imply the same experience. Modern New Testament study suggests that promises attributed to Jesus in his lifetime were not so much the verbatim records of those who were present as inspired rearrangements which take into account the experiences of Christians after the resurrection and cast the Lord's teaching into forms which help the needs and concerns of the growing Church. Thus the promise 'Where two or three are gathered in my name, there am I in the midst of them' appears in a church setting familiar to readers born too late to have known Jesus in the flesh.[92] It is the same with those passages in St John where Jesus claims himself to be the truth, and commits to the community the word of truth.[93] Similarly, the promises of the Comforter who, when Jesus is no longer with them, will lead the disciples into all truth and enable them to live and remain in the truth were all validated in later experience.[94] So, too, with St Paul's 'gospel', which is God's word of power[95] and which may never be falsified.[96] In 1 Timothy the Church is called 'the pillar and ground of truth'.[97] The underlying conviction is the same, expressed in many ways: the authority which the disciples recognized in Jesus is present still within the Church. It is the truth; and the truth cannot fail.

Jesus once said, 'He who hears you hears me, and he who rejects you rejects me, and he who rejects me rejects him who sent me.' That saying was of particular importance in the early Church. I quoted it from Luke 10.16, where it closes a section denouncing certain villages that had rejected the Seventy whom Jesus had sent on a temporary mission. But the saying can stand on its own and with very slight variations it appears in several contexts and in all four Gospels.[98] That suggests that it was a favourite text in the earliest Church and it is not hard to see why. It commits Jesus to the actions which his people would take in obedience to his command to preach the gospel. Christians who heard the accounts of Jesus read at their insecure worship behind locked doors would take great encouragement from those words. Only the authority of Jesus enabled them to believe that the powers of death would not prevail against them.

Previous sections of this chapter have considered many of the common objections to the belief in infallibility. Infallibility as Catholics understand it makes sense only if church teaching grows by development rather than by evolution. It is fatuous unless the faith is something given by divine revelation. If infallibility is accepted, there must be a magisterium of some kind through which it may be expressed. But if all these considerations are decided in favour of a Catholic view of the faith, the question still remains: are the distinctive papal claims to infallibility acceptable, or should we look for a different means for its expression? Is Peter to be found in the papacy? One other aspect needs discussion before we start to answer that question.

8
JURIDICAL AND PASTORAL

The draconic dogmatic and disciplinary dictatorship of the Roman see, as it is now and has been for many centuries exercised, is simply one manifestation of the fact . . . that Rome has allowed the juridical aspect of the Church to dominate the sacramental, so that the very lineaments of the Body of Christ have been distorted.[99]

So Dr Mascall wrote with his usual clarity of thought and language. His criticism is the more serious for being made in the course of a warm defence of Catholic Christianity. For him, it is simply the intrusive and overweening juridicism which prevents the recognition of Roman claims. And that fault lies deep enough to distort the whole. Dr Mascall's words were published in 1958. They expressed the feelings of many who even then longed for reunion with Rome. The Vatican Council has dominated the years since Dr Mascall wrote and the Roman Church has undergone costly self-examination. Has Dr Mascall's criticism in consequence lost some of its force?

Jurisdiction and related notions put most non-Roman Christians on their guard. The very ring of the words is alien. They suggest compulsion and quicken images which trigger all the latent hostility to 'popery'. Evangelicals equate them with legalism, the denial of gospel freedom similar to the Judaizing which Paul castigated when it threatened the churches of Galatia.[100] So formidable an array of theological and emotional reactions demands careful definition and rigorous argument.

Definition is easy. The word jurisdiction 'as currently employed is a legal term derived from the Roman juridical tradition'.[101] It has to do with the power and authority of administration and control. In its original context it is a political matter, for it concerned the proper relationships between people within a sovereign state. The Church as it developed within human society took on many characteristics of a political state and took over some of the machinery which kept the state going. By the end of the Middle Ages the Western Church was in the curious position of being at once a state in its own right with its sovereign ruling in Rome, one among many, and a supernational, supernatural power claiming the spiritual allegiance of all other states, their rulers and their subjects. Roman Catholics as well as others question the appropriateness of continuing this political model of church authority when the Church has become once more a voluntary society within the politically organized world. Equally open to question is whether Jesus really conferred on Peter 'true and proper jurisdiction' over the whole Church in the sense demanded by those legal terms.

The fact we must keep in mind is that those were the terms in which the First Vatican Council framed the constitution *Pastor Aeternus*, and that they are therefore built into the modern Roman Catholic teaching on the Church. We consider the substance of this teaching, and its development since Vatican II, in the next chapter. Our concern now is with the compatibility of juridical language and concepts with those of biblical and sacramental theology. Dr Mascall, in the study of the matter already quoted, produced evidence that the current Roman emphasis forced the most sensitive Roman Catholic expositions of the Church to contradict themselves. He found, indeed, a contradiction in Pope Pius XII's encyclical *Mystici Corporis Christi*,[102] a foundation work. The encyclical opened splendidly with a statement of the Church as the Body of Christ, 'the organic entity in which the human race which corporately fell in Adam is corporately restored in Christ and in which the sacraments are the vital organs by which life in Christ is communicated and sustained'.[103] But when he came to treat of papal authority, Pope Pius's argument subtly changed. Pressed by the need to do justice to Vatican I, he replaced the organic, sacramental language about the Church in this world and beyond by a vocabulary which effectively equated the Catholic Church with that section of it that is militant here in earth. Dr Mascall pointed to a similar contradiction in two writers on the Church who stressed its sacramental nature, Karl Adam[104] and Dom Columba Cary-Elwes.[105] As things then stood, he suggests, such contradiction could not be avoided.

But all that was before Vatican II. Has that Council's

emphasis on the Church as the pilgrim people of God restored a proper balance between the juridical and the other elements in the doctrine of the Church? Dr Hans Küng for one thinks not. He calls attention to a 'bad join' in *Lumen Gentium* very like that which Dr Mascall found in *Mystici Corporis Christi*. It occurs at the end of chapter II. 'In the chapters on the mystery of the Church and the people of God, the language is above all biblical, pastoral, ecumenical; in Chapter III it becomes juridical, institutional, disciplinary, Roman, though with an occasional touch of unction.'[106]

That summary seems a little unkind and its antitheses are too sharply drawn. We saw earlier that the pastoral image of ministry implies an institution. The shepherd has his flock; and, as the image was used in the Old Testament, the king's reponsibility is to rule his people. Both relationships imply an institution whose health and safety demands its own discipline. Can that exist without a juridical element? Whether it should be modelled on Roman law is another question; but although 'hard cases make bad law', a little unction makes the wheels revolve more smoothly.

It is possible to condemn the juridical element too sweepingly. Even at the First Vatican Council there were those who insisted that *Pastor Aeternus* must be interpreted pastorally. A future Cardinal Archbishop of Cologne derived the notion of *plenitudo potestas* not from the analogy with worldly powers but from Christ's commission to Peter.[107] An Italian bishop, the official reporter for chapter 3 of *Pastor Aeternus*, argued that just as individual bishops are commissioned to feed the particular flocks committed to them, so the pope is commissioned to feed the entire flock of Christ.[108] Recalling these instances, Fr Avery Dulles suggests that the pope's universal jurisdiction as Peter's successor is very different from the 'jurisdiction exercised by a patriarch or metropolitan over some group of churches as a matter of human or ecclesiastical law'.[109] If Vatican II's development of its predecessor could be continued along lines which emphasize the pastoral, and so ultimately sacramental, nature of papal jurisdiction, the positive value of that notion would be more apparent.

Father Dulles cites the view of Cornelius Ernst[110] that Vatican I narrowed the debate unnecessarily, creating the seeds of future trouble, when it ranged a 'primacy of honour' against a 'primacy of jurisdiction', so that the term 'jurisdiction' was made to exclude a mere primacy of honour. But the two do not necessarily exclude each other. Neither of them quite conveys to the present day the particular flavour of the primacy conveyed by the words of Jesus preserved in Matthew 16.16–19. Ernst suggested the term 'ontological' or, in a broad sense, 'sacramental'. 'In a sacramental view of primacy,' Dulles concludes, 'the notion of papal power moves away from jurisdiction in the legal sense towards a style of leadership based on charism and moral authority.'[111] Ernst claimed that in the writings of Leo the Great, so often seen as the architect of the medieval papacy, sacramental themes of primacy were more important than the juridical ones which later predominated. Like so many others, he saw in John XXIII's brief pontificate an example of the original unity between the various strands in primacy.

The connection between doctrine and canon law is hard to express satisfactorily. The Church is necessarily an institution within human history, tracing itself back to the time of the apostles. As such, it must have its organs of self-preservation, its customs, its rules. Yet, as Mascall reminds us, it is not only an historical institution; it is also a foretaste, a first instalment of the Kingdom of God which ends and transcends history. It is therefore not possible to devise an institutional description of the Church which will cover the whole mystery. But the description must include language suited to its historical situation as the pilgrim people on the march. Political, legal, even sociological categories will therefore have a part. But they must not be used to suggest that the Church as an historical community is a community enclosed in history; it is open to forces from beyond. In that indeed the Church is not alone; history itself is open to forces from beyond. But the Church as the focus for the redemptive transformation of humanity through its Lord may look for a greater intensity of signs from beyond. Those signs will not abolish or overthrow the historical, institutional features, but they will bring out their true meaning. The Church's confidence in thus looking for signs goes back to the Lord's command at the Last Supper and to the experience of the apostles on the road to Emmaus when he was made known to them in the breaking of bread.

'Where Christ is, there is the Church.' The ancient maxim expresses the essence of the sacramental view. It captures the distinctive Christian experience; and since one of the great charters establishing it is the Lord's promise in Matthew 18.15–20, it cannot be held to exclude a juridical element, if by that is meant the upholding of pastoral discipline.

5
Recognizing Peter in
the Papacy

The Protestant who tries to understand from within Roman Catholic teaching on the papacy is faced with a daunting task. I wrote at the beginning of the previous chapter about the need to suspend judgement until we have been able by empathy to share something of the Catholic outlook. But it is a matter of intellect as well as of attitude. So many misunderstandings are possible through failing to perceive the different associations which the same word may have for different people. I have therefore gone to some length to expound the chief elements in the Catholic dogma, so far as possible in the spirit of those for whom it belongs to the word of life. But the time comes for ending the suspension of judgement. Questions must be asked which will determine on which side of the fence we stand. Are the papal claims true? The pope claims to sit in the chair of Peter so that the Lord's words to Peter speak now to him. We remember the profile of Peter recovered through New Testament study. Looking at the papacy today, is it possible to discern beneath the trappings and accretions of history the impression of a Galilean face; the face of weak, sinful, and repentant man, a fisherman who turned shepherd and became martyr, one to whom the deepest truths about God and man have been revealed, truths which he receives and confesses, guards and passes on?

. . . We [i.e. Pope Pius IX], adhering faithfully to the tradition received from the beginning of the Christian faith – with a view to the glory of our Divine Saviour, the exaltation of the Catholic religion, and the safety of Christian peoples (the Sacred Council approving), teach and define as a dogma divinely revealed: That the Roman Pontiff, when he speaks *ex cathedra* (that is, when – fulfilling the office of Pastor and Teacher of all Christians – on his supreme Apostolical authority, he defines a doctrine concerning faith or morals to be held by the Universal Church), through the divine assistance promised him in blessed Peter, is endowed with that infallibility, with which the Divine Redeemer has willed that His Church – in defining doctrine concerning faith or morals – should be equipped: And therefore, that such definitions of the Roman Pontiff of themselves – and not by virtue of the consent of the Church – are irreformable. If anyone shall presume (which God forbid!) to contradict this our definition; let him be anathema.[1]

That is the dogma as it appeared in the constitution *Pastor Aeternus* promulgated in the fourth session of the First Vatican Council, 1870. Before considering it in detail we shall look at the Petrine office, so called, as it has been developed recently.

'Follow me: from henceforth you shall catch men.' 'When you are converted, strengthen your brethren.' 'Simon, son of Jonah, do you love me? Feed my sheep.' It can never be a light matter to be the rock on which the Church is built. The promises and commissions which Peter received implied that he was a picked man, the leader. But he was not picked for his personal advantage or pleasure or peace of mind. All his honours were the badges of service. The words 'minister' and 'ministry' are menial words, a fact which politicians perhaps neglect more than clergymen. A minister is a servant and his glory is to serve those among whom he is appointed.

Servus servorum Dei, slave of the slaves of God, is among the pope's ancient titles. Yet servanthood cannot be said to be an image which the papacy has notably projected. One of the blessings which John XXIII bestowed on the Church during his short pontificate was to embody that image. Pope John was fortunate, of course, to live at a time when mass media could spread a reputation overnight. But it was no gimmick of publicity which turned this elderly career diplomat into Good Pope John. To the Catholic world he was most eminently a father, the Holy Father. The non-Catholic world suddenly received a vision of what papacy might be. Ecumenical theologians, wrestling in hidden places with the need to find a way of discussing papacy which would make Christian sense to the non-Catholic, became aware of a pope who almosty miraculously put his finger on points of common Christian concern: speaking eternal truth in contemporary terms, modernizing without losing essentials, commending a faith which united instead of divided, serving the world at points of need. Above all, serving. If the pope had a role which many could accept, it was to be the servant of God's servants. A primacy of service is one element in the papacy over which Protestants, groping after a meaning for that remarkable institution, find little difficulty. It will be one of the planks in any wider acceptance of the papacy. But how much weight can it bear?

A chief effect of Pope John's pontificate has been to restore to the hieratic figure a true humanity. St Peter at one end has been frozen in stained glass, the pope at the other cocooned in protocol. It has all seemed remote from the emphases of St Peter's own pastoral letter: 'So I exhort the elders among you, as a fellow elder . . . Tend the flock of God that is in your charge, not by constraint but willingly, not for shameful gain but eagerly, not as domineering over those in your charge, but by being examples to the flock. And when the chief Shepherd is manifested you will obtain the unfading crown of glory.'[2] Since Pope John it has been easier to connect those words of St Peter's with the ministry of his alleged successors.

Close to the heart of the matter lies the first of St Peter's antitheses: 'not by constraint but willingly'. Christian ministry at its best shows a grace and a delight even where it is most demanding. St Peter's phrase recalls St Paul's mood when he ended a catalogue of hardships endured in the cause, 'and, apart from other things, there is the daily pressure upon me of my anxiety for all the churches. Who is weak, and I am not weak? Who is made to fall, and I am not indignant!' Paul is aware that he is boasting. 'If I must boast, I will boast of the things that show my weakness.'[3] He refers to some mysterious 'thorn in the flesh' – epilepsy has been suggested. Three times he had prayed to have it removed; 'But he said to me, "My grace is sufficient for you, for my power is made perfect in weakness." I will all the more gladly boast of my weaknesses, that the power of Christ may rest upon me.'[4] That is the mood of authentic Christian ministry. Its presence in the papacy will do much to increase the credibility of that office.

Since Pope John it has been easier to consider the papacy in those terms. Hans Urs von Balthasar writes illuminatingly of those forbidding words which end chapter 3 of Vatican I's Constitution on the Church: 'If anyone says that the Roman Pontiff has only an office of inspection or direction and not a sovereign power of jurisdiction over the whole Church, . . .'[5] 'It is astonishing', he says, 'to reflect that for a century a man has been invested with such power and has not yet broken under his burden.'[6] Von Balthasar's assessment of 'the Pope today' combines most sensitively the declarations of Vatican I with the qualifications of Vatican II. More radical Catholic theologians believe that Vatican II began a process of modifying its predecessor's position which must continue drastically if the Church is really to come to terms with today and they were often critical of Pope Paul and his advisers for slowing the pace of change. Peter Hebblethwaite, for example, finds it paradoxical that the Pope's exalted conception of his office should be matched by deep personal humility. In a chapter of *The Runaway Church* headed 'The agony of Pope Paul', he writes 'Diplomacy was for so long his milieu.' It was, of course, Pope John's too. 'The papacy is his vocation and cross. He has many times spoken of the need to combine the spirit of St Paul with that of St Peter . . ., the Petrine principle of order, stability, continuity, and firmness with the Pauline principle of dynamism, energy, and Christ-centred creativity.'[7] But, despite his chosen name, the Petrine principle triumphed. Perhaps, though this is not Mr Hebblethwaite's reaction, it was right that it should. The situation has not changed since Pope Paul's death.

Hans Küng, that stern critic of Vatican I and its legacy, is as firm on the need for maintaining the distinctively Petrine ministry at the centre of the Church as he is discerning about the human demands which that ministry makes on its holder. He poses the question: 'Would the real Peter have recognized himself in the picture, built up for him in Rome?'[8] Distortion may have entered that picture, he suggests, as Petrine ministry came to be presented in terms of Petrine power; its correction will come when the papacy voluntarily surrenders elements of power in the interest of extending its service. Nor is that mere wishful thinking – the possibility of a Vatican II for all its short-comings following on Vatican I can be matched by examples earlier in history of great pastoral popes following a series of very power-conscious predecessors. Dr Küng goes back to the New Testament to show how in each of the three great Petrine passages the promise of Peter's greatness is associated with a reprimand, for each promise carries its own temptation.[9]

> The greatness of the temptation corresponds to the greatness of the mission. Who could measure the enormous burden of respon-sibility, care, suffering, and anguish which lies on the Petrine ministry if its holder *really* wants to be rock, really key-bearer, really shepherd at the service of the Church as a whole. For the time is long past when Leo X, contemporary of Luther, could talk about enjoying the papacy as a gift of God.[10]

Dr Küng does not directly answer his question whether the original would recognize himself in what Rome has made of his office. But his implication seems clear. 'In all the toil and tribulation involved in this ministry, in all the feeling of being misunderstood and in all the holder's awareness of his un-suitability, how often faith will be inclined to waver, love to fail, the hope of overcoming the gates of the underworld to fade.'[11] Peter's face is clear. Küng's conclusion does much to cure the Evangelical of any lurking notion that the papacy represents the climax in a legalistic perversion of the gospel: 'This ministry more than any other is thrown back on the grace of the Lord.'[12]

2

The great achievement of the First Vatican Council was to locate apostolic authority fair and square in the person of the bishop of Rome as St Peter's successor. Roman Catholic teaching on this point is often condemned as uncompromising, but it has the ad-vantage of dispelling previous uncertainty. Gallicanism with its savour of absolute monarchy is no longer an option. *Pastor Aeternus* supplies the solid, unambiguous teaching which theologians may go ahead to clarify.

The dogma of papal infallibility was held to carry inescapable implications. These were brought to a fine point in the canons which concluded the three chapters of *Pastor Aeternus* which precede the actual definition.

> If anyone says that the blessed apostle Peter was not constituted by Christ the Lord as the Prince of all the Apostles and the visible head of the whole Church militant; or that he received immediately and directly from the same Jesus Christ our Lord a primacy of honour only and not of true and proper jurisdiction, let him be anathema.[13]

> If anyone says that it is not from the institution of Christ the Lord himself, or by divine law, that St Peter has perpetual successors in the primacy over the whole Church; or that the Roman Pontiff is not St Peter's successor in the same primacy, let him be anathema.[14]

> If anyone says that the Roman Pontiff has only the office of inspection or direction, but not the full and supreme power of jurisdiction in the whole Church, not only in matters which pertain to faith and morals, but also to those which pertain to the discipline and government of the Church throughout the whole world; or if anyone says that he has the greater part but not the complete fullness of this supreme power; or if anyone says that this power is not ordinary and immediate over each and every church and each and every shepherd and faithful, let him be anathema.[15]

Here we have papal authority at its starkest and least attractive. There seems little room for manoeuvre. You either accept these statements or you do not; and their tone encourages those who are not Roman Catholics to reject them at once and with relief.

That reaction is superficial. It ignores the difficulties which many loyal Catholics themselves find, and the tradition which has been established of preserving the reality which they guard while searching for better ways of expressing that reality. It is, in fact, possible to tell the baby from the bathwater. To quote again that most thoughtful theologian H. U. von Balthasar:

> If one examines – not without the sensation of terror – this old text of a century ago, one can see the cracks in the supporting piers, cracks due to basic errors of design, and one is filled with a sense of fear for every vehicle which one can see during that century driving over this bridge of San Luis Rey.[16]

The constitution *Pastor Aeternus* was, to continue von Balthasar's metaphor, an emergency structure hastily run up at a time of crisis. It was designed to be a major part of that defence which the nineteenth-century Church erected against the assaults of secular liberalism. It was the answer to the loss of the Papal States. It was also a riposte to the conservative catholicism of some contemporary states which were willing to protect the papacy at the price of controlling their national Church. More profoundly, it was a decisive but moderate intervention in a debate which had been smouldering since the time of Dante, over whether pope or General Council was finally the higher authority. Seen amid the cross-currents of mid-nineteenth-century opinion, *Pastor Aeternus* surprises less by its defiance than by its moderation. If the heirs of Gallican or Febronian[17] state control felt excluded by it, there were many other Catholics who would like it to have gone very much further in freeing the pope from all human control.

One structural crack which alarms many is the oversimplification of history. It is seen in the willingness to interpret gospel sayings in categories derived from Roman secular law. It appears also in the fundamentalistic understanding of the gospel narrative which such treatment implies. Did Jesus really stand in Galilee and constitute Peter the visible head of the entire Church militant? The body of the text summed up in the first 'anathema' seems to read John 1.42, Matthew 16.15f, and John 21.15f in just that way. It implies that Jesus foresaw the course of history with the need for the Church to continue as an organization with a particular power-structure. Is it possible to string those three texts together and define their consolidated meaning in terms of a later church situation? One text is from St Matthew's Gospel and two from St John's, both highly developed works with distinct perspectives, intentions, and backgrounds. Should not the texts be interpreted first from the place which they occupy in their own Gospel? It is not respect for the Scriptures which scans them for infallible proof-texts to support extraneous dogmatic positions.

But to dismiss *Pastor Aeternus* on the score of its defective biblical method is surely to fall into its own error of interpreting an historical text unhistorically. Such defect of method is common to almost all theological work done before the end of the last century, and of itself it invalidates *Pastor Aeternus* no more than any other precritical theology. Today's more sensitive approach has its roots in the liberalism against which Vatican I was fighting. Its practitioners then were mostly opposed to all dogmatic religion. That historical criticism might actually further the Catholic faith was almost unthinkable. The example of contemporary Protestant communities suggested that to adopt historical methods was to take the first step in a Gadarene descent which ended in the loss of all objective belief.

The struggle to claim historical criticism as a tool valuable in Catholic self-understanding is not entirely over yet.[18] The Modernist controversy of the first part of this century belongs to history, but it was not until 1943 that Catholic scholars received the freedom from dogmatic control in their researches which other students of Christian origins had long taken for granted. Pope Pius XII is not often considered an architect of Vatican II, but his encyclical *Divino Afflante Spiritu* (1943) provided the great charter of modern biblical study, enabling Catholic scholars at last to take part in the growing interchurch community of biblical scholarship. In 1955, the Pontifical Biblical Commission 'clarified' the status of many decrees which it had issued during the anti-Modernist period, which were henceforth of historical interest only. In 1964 the Commission issued an Instruction which assumed that the Gospels are not literal or chronological accounts of what the Lord said or did; a stage characterized by the preaching of the apostles came between the life and times of Jesus and the work of the canonical Gospel writers. That framework allows the view, for example, that the Christology of the early Church was developed after the resurrection, instead of stemming directly from the earthly Jesus's teaching about himself. It allowed also that 'when the Lord was orally explaining his doctrine, he followed the modes of reasoning and of exposition which were in vogue at the time'.

Protestant scholars may well find much to learn from an approach which finds no contradiction between a thoroughly human interpretation of the words of Scripture and a belief that they should be taken to convey the word of God:

For the truth of the story is not at all affected by the fact that the Evangelists relate the words and deeds of the Lord in a different order, and express his sayings not literally but differently, while preserving (their) sense. For, as St Augustine says, 'It is quite probable that each Evangelist believed it to have been his duty to recount what he had to in that order in which it pleased God to suggest it to his memory. . . .'[19]

The underlying philosophy of Scripture insists that 'the doctrine and life of Jesus were not reported for the sole purpose of being remembered, but were "preached" so as to offer the Church a basis of faith and of morals'. Dr Raymond E. Brown calls attention to the doctrine of biblical inerrancy in the Vatican II Constitution on Revelation, 'which has made it possible to restrict inerrancy to the essential religious affirmations of a biblical book made for the sake of our salvation'.[20] That position seems very close to that of the Sixth of the Thirty-Nine Articles of Religion.

A second crack in the structure of *Pastor Aeternus*, to return to Father von Balthasar's metaphor, is the apparent equation between a truth and the particular doctrinal form in which it is embodied. One is reminded at once of Pope John's seminal phrase at the opening of Vatican II: 'The substance of the ancient doctrine of the deposit of faith is one thing, and the way in which it is presented is another.'[21] That phrase has done more than any other to open possibilities of restatement for doctrines whose previous formulation had resulted in deadlock between Catholic and Protestant. Some must find it ironical that the most important elaboration of that liberating distinction occurs in *Mysterium Ecclesiae*,[22] the document which the Doctrinal Congregation produced in order, it is said, to refute certain of Hans Küng's views. But the real importance of *Mysterium Ecclesiae* lies in endorsing the view that all doctrinal statements are conditioned by the outlook of their own time. No longer can the strict conservative who finds the truth in every phrase of the magisterium go to the Doctrinal Congregation for support. At the other end of the scale, those who are embarrassed by a crude statement of doctrine should not reject that statement altogether, but try to correct any one-sided emphasis by drawing out its further meaning. It is a matter of interpretation where four factors are involved. The meaning of a pronouncement depends partly on the sense which the words had at the time when it was made. Secondly, 'it sometimes happens that some dogmatic truth is first expressed incompletely (but not falsely)',[23] to be more perfectly developed later. Thirdly, such pronouncements are generally made, not just to expand our understanding of truth, but in order to refute some error of the time which is distorting or threatening the truth. Finally, although the particular truth in question is to be distinguished from 'the changeable conceptions of a given epoch and can be expressed without them, nevertheless it can sometimes happen that these truths may be enunciated by the Sacred Magisterium in terms that bear traces of such conceptions'.[24] The process is thus similar to that which enables Catholic scholars to maintain that the Bible is the word of God and yet that word is in the fullest sense expressed in the words of men. To some it may seem a case of having your cake and eating it. But is that not an admirable achievement?

The way is open, therefore, for the strictest scrutiny of the most authoritative pronouncement. Correction is possible, to proceed not by rejection but by amplification. These principles may be applied to the uncompromising assertions of *Pastor Aeternus*.

It is apparent that *Pastor Aeternus* expresses the Petrine powers in terms of sovereign authority, the most urgent issue in a Church quite literally under siege. It was involved also in the internal struggle with the conciliar view that bishops in council controlled the pope, who had no authority apart from them. *Pastor Aeternus* decided that issue in the pope's favour: the extent to which his authority was shared by the bishops could not be considered objectively until the major issue was clear. A further stage in establishing the true distribution of authority opened with Vatican II's teaching on collegiality. As we shall see, this has in no way gone back on the positions of Vatican I, but has developed them by putting them in a fuller context. Finally, there is a marked difference in the 'tone' of teaching about the pope given in the two councils. Vatican I, driven by immediate needs, is juridical to the point of overshadowing all other aspects. Vatican II discusses the hierarchical structure of the Church, including of course the pope, in its place within the whole pilgrim people of God. That section of its teaching has indeed been criticized as a juridical intrusion within a sacramental understanding of the Church. But, as I have already argued,[25] the juridical element must not be denied its proper place. There will no doubt be improvements on the balance achieved by Vatican II, but the total elimination of the juridical element will not be one.

Catholic critics have not been slow to point out that it was one thing for the Council to endorse collegiality and another for that principle to take serious effect. They have traced sadly Pope Paul's apparent waning of enthusiasm for collegiality: the issue of his personal *Credo* in 1967, the *Humanae Vitae* affair, the equivocation over World Population Year. Some believed him to have become the prisoner of his own Curia, others that he was in charge to the end but less certain than before of the direction to take. Pope John Paul I held office too briefly to show how his less formal style might affect relations between pope and bishops. Pope John Paul II has so far made it clear that collegial consultation does not mean discharging his office by accepting majority decisions.

Collegiality as its name implies views the teaching office of the Church as essentially corporate. Chapter 3 of *Lumen Gentium*, the main source for Vatican II teaching on the hierarchy, stresses its continuity with Vatican I:

> Jesus Christ, the eternal pastor, set up the holy Church by entrusting the apostles with their mission as he himself had been sent by the Father. . . . He willed that their successors, the bishops namely, should be the shepherds in his Church until the end of the world. In order that the episcopate itself, however, might be one and undivided he put Peter at the head of the other apostles, and in him he set up a lasting and visible source and foundation of the unity both of faith and of communion.[26]

Taking that teaching as established, authoritative, and true, Vatican II proceeded to its own distinctive task, namely 'to proclaim publicly and enunciate clearly the doctrine concerning bishops, successors of the apostles, who together with Peter's successor, the Vicar of Christ and the visible head of the whole Church, direct the house of the living God'.[27] Critics of the Roman Catholic Church as it emerged from the First Vatican Council often commented on the insignificant role to which the bishop had been reduced, when so many matters were reserved for decision in Rome. Vatican II determined to redress the balance.

That balance was delicate. The New Testament evidence is interpreted after the manner of Irenaeus, greatest of the very early Church Fathers. The bishops, successors to apostles, are guardians of apostolic tradition, shepherds, and teachers, so that 'whoever listens to them is listening to Christ and whoever despises them despises Christ and him who sent Christ'.[28] Christ is present in the midst of the faithful 'in the person of the bishops' and it is he who is the true operator in the bishops' appointed functions of preaching and administering the sacraments. In order to play so exalted a part, the apostles were endowed by Christ with a special outpouring of the Spirit, which is continued through the conferring of episcopal orders. 'Now, episcopal consecration confers, together with the office of sanctifying, the duty also of teaching and ruling, which, however, of their very nature can be exercised only in hierarchical communion with the head and members of the college.'[29] The early Christian centuries are called upon to substantiate the collegiate nature of the episcopate, seen notably in the ready recourse to councils of bishops and to the custom of consecrating bishops at the hands of more than one of them.

Collegiality is thus firmly asserted and it is held in tension, not always easily, with papal primacy. The college of bishops has no authority unless united with Peter's successor. All bishops are the successors of the apostles as teachers and pastors, but 'the Lord made Peter alone the rock-foundation and the holder of the keys of the Church . . . and constituted him shepherd of his whole flock. . . .'[30] But the power of binding and loosing thus conferred on Peter distinctively was given also to the apostles as a whole. *Lumen Gentium* founds its teaching on collegiality on that double assignment of Christ's own authority to Peter himself and 'to the college of the apostles united to its head'. The college expresses the truly catholic variety of the Church and its unity in a single flock under one head. Within that unity the bishops, 'whilst loyally respecting the primacy and pre-eminence of their head, exercise their own proper authority for the good of their faithful, indeed even for the good of the whole Church, the organic structure and harmony of which are strengthened by the continued influence of the Holy Spirit'.[31] An ecumenical council exercises most notably the supreme authority of the college over the Church, but its true ecumenical status depends on recognition by Peter's successor.

Tension between the place of pope and bishops comes out in the relation between shepherds and flock. The pope as Peter's successor

> is the perpetual and visible source and foundation of the unity both of the bishops and of the whole company of the faithful. The individual bishops are the visible source and foundation of unity in their own particular churches, which are constituted after the model of the universal Church; it is in these and formed out of them that the one and unique Catholic Church exists.[32]

A bishop looks after the particular section of the one flock assigned to him, not other local churches or the Church universal; though in a non-jurisdictional manner all bishops are bound to contribute to the well-being of the whole Mystical Body. The bishop's mission is to preach the gospel as well as to feed the flock. In discussing the spread of the gospel, *Lumen Gentium* mentions the groupings of local churches with their own customs that have resulted, in some cases organized into patriarchates with their own internal relationships. They all add to the rich diversity of the one Church. But however important a bishop may be, he does not in himself enjoy infallibility. Even so, bishops who are not personally infallible may proclaim infallibly the doctrine of Christ when, in communion with the see of Peter, they agree on a particular matter relating to faith or morals. There is, however, an important difference. The infallibility in the bishops' teaching lies in the deposit of revelation which they interpret correctly; whereas the 'Roman Pontiff, head of the college of bishops, enjoys this in virtue of his office, when, as supreme pastor and teacher of all the faithful – who confirms his brethren in the faith (cf. Luke 22.32) – he proclaims in an absolute decision a doctrine pertaining to faith or morals'.[33]

Tension between pope and bishop in the pastoral sphere is implied by a passage which interrupts an eloquent and extended exposition of the bishop's sacramental function in the local church. The pastoral charge is entrusted to the bishop fully. He is not to be regarded as the Roman Pontiff's vicar. Consequently his authority, 'far from being damaged by the supreme and universal power, is rather much defended, upheld, and strengthened by it, since the Holy Spirit preserves unfailingly that form of government which was set up by Christ the Lord in his Church'.[34] That reassurance is buttressed by a reference to *Pastor Aeternus*. Vatican II must be shown to be drawing out more fully its predecessor's teaching, not subverting it.

Did Vatican II manage to restore the balance tilted against the bishops by the anti-Gallican concern of Vatican I? Hans Küng for one has answered with a resounding No. The basic problem remains that papal absolutism developed by the reforming popes of the eleventh century and never relinquished. 'For all its solemn and pious talk and decisions on collegiality,' Küng declares, 'Vatican II did not succeed in making headway against this papal absolutism.'[35] He has no hesitation in accusing the progressive majority of lazy compromise with the curial minority. They managed to extend a Vatican I-type view of infallibility to the episcopate but did not tackle the problem of an effective curb on the pope when he is determined to go against advice. In any conflict, the pope has law and dogma firmly behind him. There is according to Küng one way only to check papal absolutism: to give collegiality as solidly juridical a base in ecclesiastical law as that in which the papal authority is grounded. That would mean modifying Vatican I. But it is 'the only way in which the absolute monarch – the only representative of the *ancien régime* who survived the French Revolution – might be turned into a constitutional monarch and the Roman Empire into something in the nature of a Catholic Commonwealth'.[36]

Hans Küng is a theologian of rare authority. The lucidity of his thought survives even the difficult transition from German to

English. His book *Infallible?* is both a scientific inquiry and a personal statement. It takes its place in his long struggle against curial attempts to circumscribe the theologian's proper task and its particular strictures grow out of his conviction that Pope Paul was wrong in his judgement, as well as high-handed, when he went against expert advice in issuing *Humanae Vitae* to uphold the traditional prohibition of artificial birth prevention. That is the background to his challenge to the complacency of post-Vatican II theology. What do you do if another pope should go further, carrying his personal convictions to the point of heresy, or standing alone against the whole Church?

Küng's reply is to go behind Vatican II and Vatican I alike, looking at the issues of 1870 in a longer perspective than was possible to the historical science of the time, or than was attempted at the second Council. He wishes to re-examine everything: the biblical texts in the light of historical criticism, the concepts of infallibility and magisterium, the effects of history on theological development. He believes that in-fallibility is a positive inversion of an essentially negative quality. It could not guarantee truth in the form of propositions, for historical conditioning in the use and meaning of words makes that impossible. Infallible truth indeed exists, but it belongs to God alone and any human attempt to express it once and for all can only be presumptuous.

Placing as he does a question mark beside every statement of the faith, Küng is open to the most radical restatement of doc-trine. But since he also believes that infallible truth exists, he does not stand for a thoroughgoing relativism, let alone for in-difference in matters of doctrine. The dynamic relationship between the truth of God itself, which cannot change, and the statement of it in terms which are bound to change demands constant revision. Küng wishes above all to be a theologian of the Church, which means that any theological revision must take place within the life of the Church as a living community. In-fallibility as a notion he judges inappropriate, but he would have in its place not a void but the notion of indefectibility: the Church will not be allowed to fall away beyond hope from the truth. Indefectibility is innocent of the triumphalist possibilities which have discredited infallibility in much Catholic teaching since 1870, and is a concept acceptable to Eastern Orthodox, Anglican, and many Protestant churchmen. It offers therefore ecumenical possibilities which Anglican and other Protestant reviewers have welcomed. Dr Küng's insights were developed against a notably polemical background in *Infallible?*. They are set out more positively in his magisterial *On Being a Christian*,[37] where the huge scale of the canvas throws the issues into proportion. The defensive Catholic claims have sundered the Christian world in the interests of Roman primacy. Is there, he asks, a way back from primacy understood as a primacy of domination to the more ancient primacy of service which the growing emphasis on domination displaced? He believes that there is, and he discerns its outlines in a profile of the original Peter and his three great temptations. 'Perhaps the Eastern Orthodox or Protestant Christian will be able to sympathize a little with the Catholic in his conviction that something will be lacking in his Church and perhaps in Christendom as a whole if the Petrine ministry were to disappear: something that is not inessential to the Church,' he modestly concludes.[38]

But he is too modest. He is so eager to apologize for the overbearing attitude of much conventional Catholicism that he accepts too uncritically many critical assumptions. He is unnecessarily sceptical over the value of propositions in relation to the truth, for instance – *Mysterium Ecclesiae* is here a better guide. His estimate of *Humanae Vitae* is not unchallengeable. He is too ready to assume irreconcilable conflict between juridical and pastoral components in ministry. Anyone concerned for unity between Catholic and Protestant must be grateful to Dr Küng for his fresh approach to so many ancient problems and correspondingly sad that his insistence on going behind the two Vatican Councils can only lessen his future influence as an interpreter. Perhaps the most surprising feature in the Church's formal withdrawal from him of recognition as a Catholic teacher is that it came so late; one can only hope that it will be temporary. A better path is surely to accept Vatican I, for all its historical limitations, with a commitment to further Vatican II's elucidation of the truth which its predecessor expressed in terms so heavily conditioned by the pressures of its time.

That path has already been followed, especially in groups

official and unofficial where Catholic and other inquirers work together. We have already borrowed from the Lutheran–Catholic dialogue in America.[39] Another example, at the highest level of ecclesiastical standing, is the Anglican–Roman Catholic International Commission, whose 1976 Statement *Authority in the Church*[40] carried agreement to surprising lengths and identified four areas where differences remained. They were: too much weight placed upon the three great Petrine texts; the 'divine right' language in which Vatican I spoke of Peter's successors; the claim to infallibility in teaching, especially in view of the recent Marian dogmas; and the pope's claim to universal immediate jurisdiction. We have already considered the first two. In their commentary on the Statement, *Truth and Authority*,[41] two members of the Commission, the Anglican Henry Chadwick and the Roman Catholic Edward Yarnold stress the lengths to which the popes concerned went to discover the mind of the Church before defining the two dogmas. 'More positively,' they add, 'it can be said that the magisterium was seeking to articulate with theological precision the instinctive devotion of the faithful at the request of the faithful.'[42] They point to the restraints placed upon undisciplined Marian exuberance by subsequent official teaching. More generally, the Roman authorities are notably unwilling to claim infallibility for papal pronouncements. 'It might seem, therefore, that the insistence upon papal infallibility is much ado about relatively little.'[43] Its importance lies in emphasizing the universal nature of the pope's teaching responsibilities, even if in most instances it can be held in reserve.

The pope's universal and immediate jurisdiction could well be the hardest part of his primacy to accept, for it suggests limitless interference in day-to-day affairs; but it, too, is very rarely used. The rub comes with its indirect use, through the directives of curial Congregations concerning the performance of the liturgy, the training of clergy, and such matters. The problem in fact is not jurisdiction but bureaucracy. Its seriousness as an ecumenical problem derives from a combination of exasperation over bureaucratic control and hostility towards secret decisions in matters of conscience: it conjures up all the old fears of popery. Its ecumenical value, Chadwick and

Yarnold suggest, lies in inviting 'Rome to exercise a more open and less centralized form of government and to encourage a greater measure of pluriformity in Church life'.[44]

Problems of jurisdiction arise in any arrangement which brings the Anglican communion into full communion with the Roman see. Drs Chadwick and Yarnold suggest a possible way forward.[45] The present authority of the pope includes a combination of powers held under two different titles, patriarch of the Latin Church and universal primate. Many of the ways in which his authority is felt in practice belong to his powers as patriarch rather than as universal primate. In the event of full communion between Rome and Canterbury, Canterbury might be considered as a patriarchate. In that case, any intervention necessary in an Anglican diocese would normally be made by the Anglican patriarch. 'The bishop of Rome would step in only when all else had failed.'[46]

The Petrine primacy is not merely a challenge to Christian unity, an obstacle to be overcome, as Pope Paul modestly suggested. It is a distinct and permanent element in the revelation which God made in Christ and it opens up exciting possibilities for Christian activity on a global scale. But before developing that theme we must turn to the most controversial incident since Vatican II, the episode of the encyclical *Humanae Vitae*.

3

Humanae Vitae exploded like a bomb in the summer of 1968.[47]

For some years opinion had been growing among Catholic intellectuals that a revision of sexual ethics was needed. The discovery of 'the Pill' and its widespread prescription had brought matters to a head. Why should Catholics not avail themselves of it?

The respectability of birth control was quite recent. The traditional view, held by all major Christian groups and most secular moralists, understood sexual intercourse to be essentially the means of procreation. Any other use of the sexual faculty was at best dubious. Pioneers of birth control like Marie Stopes were widely considered to be subversive of good morals. But in the years between the two World Wars, a gap widened between the standards of Church teaching on sexual morality and the standards acceptable in respectable society. Birth-control methods lost their association with illicit sexual adventure and won acceptance as a normal part of married life. The Anglican bishops, assembled for the Lambeth Conference of 1930, cautiously (and not unanimously) approved what their predecessors ten years before had roundly condemned.[48] The Vatican reacted sharply with *Casti Connubii*,[49] an encyclical in which Pope Pius XI strongly asserted traditional teaching, specifically repudiating the view that newly discovered factors had outdated the traditional position. Pius XI did, however, state clearly the right of a married couple to avail themselves of the 'safe period', in the context of responsible planning for their family. It was one thing to make use of a factor naturally provided; it was quite another to obstruct or thwart the natural course of events. So the matter rested.

Two developments in the later nineteen-fifties gave it new urgency. Widespread concern with a growing divorce rate led to a new analysis of marriage which stressed the need for fostering the personal relationship between husband and wife, in which sexual intercourse had a part quite independent of producing children. The second was the need to limit the increase in world population if the earth's resources were not to be exhausted. The revolution was complete. Birth control was no longer even faintly disreputable. It was indeed the refusal of birth control which now seemed irresponsible. Anglicans and Protestants joined with secular humanists in commending the theory and practice of family planning, a term increasingly used to mean the limitation of families. They saw no force in the Roman Catholic distinction between 'natural' and 'artificial' means. The notion of a sexual act being intrinsically right or wrong seemed remote, for the quality of such an act determined by whether it strengthened or weakened the particular human relationship. The Lambeth Conference of 1958 had among its preparatory material a report, *The Family in Contemporary Society*,[50] which must be one of the most persuasive documents of the kind ever produced. Christian and humanist celebrated the power of sex to enrich human life.

The Catholic Church was faced with an agonizing choice, to

borrow the title of Norman St John Stevas's study of the matter.[51] Was this new consensus over the priority of personal relationships in sexual morality God's word to the technological age, or was it a subtle and attractive betrayal of the divine law? Pope John deemed this burning issue better discussed in a commission of theological and medical experts than in the agenda of the Vatican Council, and Pope Paul confirmed that decision. The Council therefore avoided dealing with the subject of contraception directly, though its report on *The Church in the Modern World* (*Gaudium et Spes*) could not help touching on it.[52] The short section on marriage and the family emphasized the place of love between the partners in marriage as a good in itself as well as for the upbringing of children, which suggests the more modern emphasis. But as well as condemning abortion and infanticide, it insists that sexual behaviour in marriage is to be governed by the objective criteria of revealed law, of which the Church and not the individual conscience was the interpreter.

The Council ended in 1965 and the Commission reported to the Pope the year after. The report was secret, but was widely believed to suggest that the decision whether or not to use contraceptives should be left to the individual couple, properly prepared in conscience for responsible choice. In England Cardinal Heenan, who had been a member of the Commission, issued a pastoral letter which was taken to be a preparation for change. Catholic couples who had been using the Pill believed that their action would be officially approved.

It was not. *Humanae Vitae* classed all methods of artificial birth prevention with abortion and sterilization: contraventions of the natural law. All such practices were held in contrast to the rhythm method of confining sexual intercourse to the infertile period of a woman's cycle. The difference in principle, the encyclical asserted, was quite clear. In the one method, the couple 'rightly use a facility provided them by nature'. In all others, 'they obstruct the natural development of the generative process'.[53] The right or wrong resides in the act itself, not in the motive behind it. Elizabeth Anscombe, Professor of Philosophy in the University of Cambridge, gives a helpful analogy: forging a cheque to steal from somebody in order to get funds for a good cause. 'The intentional action, presenting a cheque we've forged, is on the face of it a dishonest action, not to be vindicated by the further good intention.'[54]

It is important to be clear about the conception of natural law. It is not invoked specifically in connection with sexual matters; it is not limited to the contrast between 'natural' and 'artificial', nor is it derived from the thought of 'unnatural vice'. It is a far deeper concept: any type of wrong action is 'against the natural law'. ' "Natural law",' writes Professor Anscombe, 'is simply a way of speaking about the whole of morality, used by Catholic thinkers because they believe the general precepts of morality are *laws* promulgated by God our Creator in the enlightened human understanding when it is thinking in general terms about what are good and what are bad actions.'[55]

Natural law does not apply only in the moral field of human behaviour. It is closely related to 'laws of nature' which may be seen in the efficient functioning of anything in the created order. That which helps it to function according to its nature is good, that which impedes it is evil. Natural law in this sense applies to individuals and to social institutions. Thus marriage is an institution where a man and a woman come together in an exclusive intimacy which provides the matrix from which life may be transmitted to the next generation. A marriage where the possibility of children is deliberately frustrated is therefore a violated marriage. A marriage is sustained by the mutual love and care of the partners, and their relationship is developed partly through its most intense physical expression, the act of coitus. Yet coitus is precisely the means by which new life is generated so that an act of coitus from which the possibility of generation is deliberately excluded is an act whose nature is violated. The act is so closely connected to its primary, biological purpose that no secondary purpose, however worthy, can oust the primary one. Thus coitus from which reproduction is deliberately excluded is wrong in itself, regardless of its setting. In technical language, it is intrinsically wrong.

The teaching of *Humanae Vitae* is the traditional Catholic teaching. Voices on all sides were hoping that the pope would vary it. 'Then', writes Professor Anscombe,

with the whole world baying at him to change, the Pope acted as

135

Peter. 'Simon, Simon,' Our Lord said to Peter, 'Satan has wanted to have you all to sift you like wheat, but I have prayed for thee that thy faith should not fail: thou, being converted, strengthen thy brethren.' Thus Paul confirmed the only doctrine which had ever appeared as the teaching of the Church on these things; and in so doing incurred the execration of the world.[56]

Professor Anscombe's able and spirited support of the encyclical represents one type of reaction. A second group was made up of those who had hoped for a change, but whose initial disappointment was replaced by loyal and eventually joyful acceptance. This attitude is well represented in an unpretentious pamphlet *Facing up to Humanae Vitae*, written by one who describes herself as 'a Catholic mother'.[57] Internal evidence shows her to be a trained nurse with a large family and a sexually demanding husband. Like Elizabeth Anscombe, she writes as a loyal and instructed Catholic, but her approach is essentially practical. She had clearly hope for a positive answer about the Pill, though not without misgivings derived from her nursing experience. Initial bewilderment and dismay were followed by relief at a definite answer to end the long uncertainties. Before it came, she had been forced back to the essentials of Catholic belief. 'How does one ordinary woman determine the will of God for her, personally? From a newspaper article, a clever Catholic on TV, a kind-hearted curate dismissed by his bishop? No; from the Holy Father, appointed by God as his Vicar, to guard and define his Divine Revelation.'[58] A process of reflection then took her through the practicalities of the situation interpreted by faith. '*Humanae Vitae* was our twentieth-century test of faith', she concludes, 'and I nearly failed.'[59]

A third group were those who did not believe that *Humanae Vitae* solved permanently the problem to which it was addressed, but who yet remained within the Roman Catholic Church. They varied between those who accepted the decision as a matter of obedience but who looked upon the question as in the long term still open so that they could hope and work towards a better solution later; and those who continued to practise or (in the case of priests) to condone the use of contraceptives by those who in conscience believed it to be right. We have already considered the opinions of Dr Hans Küng; Mr St John Stevas dedicated his book to him 'with admiration for his courageous Christian witness and fidelity to the Catholic and Roman Church'. Peter Hebblethwaite's narrative of events since the Council, *The Runaway Church*, displays a similar attitude. An important side effect of *Humanae Vitae*, indeed, has been to articulate a new form of 'critical loyalty' to the Roman Catholic Church which deserves a chapter to itself.

A fourth group consists of those who found in *Humanae Vitae* evidence that the Church was not the guardian of truth which it claimed to be, and who therefore left the Church altogether.

It is now more than twelve years since this fateful encyclical was issued. The passage of time has given room for reflection. The first observation which must be made is that *Humanae Vitae* deserves to be read again. It was not, as its critics suggest, a document of panic. On the contrary, it is a considered attempt to review the newly asked questions and to give the faithful an answer which will enable them to live in the modern world without doing violence to the historic faith. In so doing, it discusses the relation between the authority of the Church's magisterium and that of experts in various fields of knowledge, theologians included. Doctrinal questions are considered in a perspective which relates immediate problems to the totality of human well-being which is only to be achieved by faithfulness to God's design. Only then does it deal with the regulation of birth, in a form which distinguishes, on the basis of the earlier argument, between lawful and unlawful ways of control. The doctrinal section ends with the Church's role in the matter.

The third part consists of pastoral directives. That on 'mastery of self' cuts clean across many widespread secular notions of the place which sexual activity should occupy in people's lives. It is perhaps pitched in too low a key, but its challenge is one that few Christians could with integrity reject. The Pope speaks realistically to educators and reminds the rulers of the nations that *Humanae Vitae* is misread if it is taken to imply a departure from the concern for human well-being expressed in his other encyclical *Populorum Progressio*.

Perhaps the least regarded section of the encyclical is that addressed to men of science. The Pope had earlier stressed that he was not condemning birth control as such. He endorses the modern concern for responsible parenthood. The birth control which is unacceptable is that which overthrows natural process. Scientists therefore are urged to inquire further into that process so as to

> 'elucidate better the conditions favourable to a lawful regulation of procreation' [a quotation from Vatican II's *Gaudium et Spes*]. It is supremely desirable, and this was also the mind of Pius XII, that medical science should by the study of natural rhythms succeed in determining a sufficiently secure basis for the chaste limitation of offspring.[60]

If the cycle could be relied upon, measures for its suspension would be far less attractive.

Another undervalued paragraph concerns the 'grave consequences of artificial birth control'. Despite ridicule, the arguments, like a good port, have matured well. Is it not true that marital fidelity is valued less highly than it used to be in our society as a whole, and are not adulterous adventures facilitated by the Pill? More difficult to assess is the warning that 'a man who grows accustomed to the use of contraceptive methods may forget the reverence due to a woman, and, disregarding her physical and emotional equilibrium, reduce her to being a mere instrument for the satisfaction of his own desires, no longer considering her as his partner whom he should surround with care and affection',[61] but it does not seem unlikely. It certainly cannot be dismissed as revealing 'a celibate's view of sexual pleasure "for its own sake" as an abandoned whoopee of mind-blowing selfishness', to use Peter Hebblethwaite's splendid phrase.[62] Further, the warning of draconian political use of birth control reads if anything more chillingly than it did twelve years ago. And finally on this point, doubts over the medical side effects of the Pill (not mentioned in the encyclical) have if anything increased over the last decade.

Humanae Vitae is sometimes said to represent a retreat from the more progressive outlook of Vatican II, in particular from the position maintained in the Pastoral Constitution on *The Church in the Modern World* (*Gaudium et Spes*). Careful reading of that document makes me think otherwise. The chapter on marriage and the family is indeed admirable. As a 'pastoral' constitution it is written with more warmth than the encyclical, but the arguments are the same in both. It is true that the Council Fathers, in view of the sitting commission, did not pronounce specifically on birth control. But they followed an unequivocal demand for married chastity with the flat assertion: 'In questions of birth regulation the sons of the Church, faithful to these principles, are forbidden to use methods disapproved of by the teaching authority of the Church in its interpretation of the divine law.'[63]

Gaudium et Spes and *Humanae Vitae* take their place in a series of pronouncements giving teaching relevant to married life in a period of social change. The Catholic Theological Society of America mounted an elaborate programme of study whose report *Human Sexuality: New Directions in Catholic Thought*[64] contains a convenient selection of extracts from official documents. The modern period began, as we have seen, in 1930, when Pius XI issued his encyclical *Casti Connubii* in reply to the qualified acceptance of birth control by the Lambeth Conference of that year. The Anglican offence was to admit that under certain circumstances 'other methods' of avoiding parenthood than abstinence from intercourse were legitimate. The Pope, while insisting that nothing could turn something intrinsically against nature into something conformable to nature and morally good, unambiguously approved 'natural' birth control.

The American report traced in Pius XI's encyclical the influence of early twentieth-century Catholic theologians who had emphasized the personalist values in their teaching on marriage. One result was to loosen the rigid hierarchy of values in marriage whereby what the Anglican Book of Common Prayer called the 'mutual society, help, and comfort' of husband and wife was subordinated to their biological function of carrying forward the species. *Casti Connubii* revealed 'a keen awareness and support of the dual purpose of sexuality' (unitive and procreative) ' – a giant step forward from the narrowly pro-creative framework of the earliest centuries'.[65] But the two had yet to be integrated.

The decisive step towards that integration was taken neither by *Gaudium et Spes*, which emphasized the personalist element, nor by *Humanae Vitae* with is reassertion of natural law and intrinsic values. A possible way forward appeared with the *Declaration on Certain Questions concerning Sexual Ethics* issued by the Sacred Congregation for the Doctrine of the Faith in 1975.[66] Like *Mysterium Ecclesiae*, the *Declaration* lays the ground for reform which advances from the past without denying it. Uncompromising in its condemnation of pre-marital sex, homosexual relationships, and masturbation, the Declaration understands sexuality to be rooted in the very nature of the human person and important to growth at every stage of being, and not merely in the context of marriage. So large an understanding of sex, the American report suggests, can go behind the sharp choice between procreation and pleasure and carry the personalist approach towards an integrated view.[67]

The affair of *Humanae Vitae* has shown the role of the pope in a world of experts, and especially the relationship between theologians and the magisterium. The pattern is clear. A particular pope, faced with the demand for authoritative guidance in a new situation, submits the matter to expert advisers. They set about it in their proper way and eventually present their report. The pope reflects on this along with other considerations ancient and modern and no doubt prays about it, agonizes over it, for only he can decide. Eventually he is certain enough to come out with his decision. He thanks his experts and dismisses them; they have done their job. He too has done his. He is not bound by the advice of even the greatest expert and cannot evade his responsibility. The voice of the people is strong, but the Church is no more a democracy than a meritocracy. He, Peter, has the responsibility of the keys. That particular matter will not in this instance be loosed. He may be wrong, he does not claim infallibility, later developments may suggest some modification, but at the moment the situation is unchanged. Peter speaks and the people of God have a provisional certainty around which they may order their lives.

Petrine ministry is essentially pastoral. Revelation is received and guarded in order to provide food for the flock. Peter is not necessarily a brilliant theologian. Indeed the historical Peter did not always seem to understand the implications of the faith which he was inspired to confess. It is possible at times to label the Petrine teaching dull, compared with that of other teachers, pedestrian. But

> Auream quisquis mediocritatem
> diligit tutus. . . .[68]

The caution of *Humanae Vitae* guards the faithful against the tyranny of the theologian who wishes to restate the faith in accordance with the latest – and no doubt passing – phase of scholarship. The prophet and the scholar are of the greatest value in the Church, but their task is to service the magisterium, not to control it. *Humanae Vitae* is not the last word that will be spoken on its subject, but true progress will come by going forward from it, not by ignoring it and going another way. This seems to have been the conclusion of the Synod of Bishops in 1980.

4

However *Humanae Vitae* may appear in the light of history, the controversy surrounding it has had an unexpected result. It has turned upside down Protestant ideas of what papal primacy means. As the Presbyterian Robert McAfee Brown put it, the response

> has demythologized a certain view of papal authority that has been a vast ecumenical stumbling-block, and reinstituted a view that Catholics, in making moral decisions, take into account Scripture, conscience, their own devotional life, and a wide view of tradition, in addition to the strictures of a single document.[69]

He gives his opinion that many Protestants, Anglicans, and Orthodox could live happily with the view of papal authority now held by many Catholics.

The notion of critical loyalty was not unknown in the Catholic Church before Vatican II. In different ways Baron von Hügel and Father Teilhard de Chardin exemplified men whose prophetic vision brought them into conflict with the prevailing style of theology. Several of the men behind the new thinking of Vatican II – Congar, Bouyer, de Lubac – suffered at the hands of the Curia and accepted it meekly before being recognized as men through whose insights the received tradition took on extended meaning. But until the *Humanae Vitae* affair, such critical loyalty appeared temporary, exceptional, and even eccentric. Critics had been rebels and had submitted or left the Church.

If one element may be selected to point the change in climate from the First to the second Vatican Council, it is the recognition that the magisterium of pope and bishops is not the only educated section of the Church. It will always be possible to distinguish *ecclesia discens* from *ecclesia docens*, but such a statement of it as that quoted above on page 65 can only sound ridiculous today. It is not possible to override the claims of personal judgement and personal conscience. Authority which resorts to authoritarian coercion ceases to be credible.

Catholics are better disposed to accept the authority of church teaching than most Protestants, because their faith includes the Church as the institution within which they encounter the things of Christ. It is natural therefore for the magisterium to articulate the truths revealed through the Holy Spirit. But for many Protestants, the Church is almost an extra to the gospel. They find it hard to enter into the position of Catholics who find themselves unable in conscience to accept points of teaching on which the Church insists, and yet remain in loyal membership. A phrase included almost casually in *Lumen Gentium* strikes them as repulsive:

> the faithful . . . are obliged to submit to their bishop's decision, made in the name of Christ, in matters of faith and morals, and to adhere to it with a ready and respectful allegiance of mind. This loyal submission of the will and intellect must be given, in a special way, to the authentic teaching authority of the Roman Pontiff. . . .[70]

They are not helped if they turn to the Latin original, for 'allegiance' and 'submission' both render the word *obsequium*; they may indeed remember Canon Sidney Smith's dictum: 'What bishops like best in their clergy is a dropping-down-deadness of manner.'[71] They may, however, be reassured. The Latin *obsequium* quite lacks the objectionable overtones of the English 'obsequious'.

That out of the way, the problem is clear. Is it possible to combine 'a ready and respectful allegiance of mind', 'a loyal submission of the will and intellect', with an integrity which must in conscience dissent where it cannot agree? Is it not more honest to opt out? A Protestant trying to understand Catholic attitudes must remember how seriously Catholic theology of the Church discourages opting out.

Fr Edward Yarnold, s.j., discusses the problem in a paper meant as the basis for parochial discussion.[72] He considers the case of a person who finds that after careful consideration he cannot follow a statement on morals made by the pope, but without formal claim to infallibility. Freedom of conscience demands respect, so there can be no rule of thumb to direct such a person. Father Yarnold offers five guidelines to help the Catholic work out his attitude. Because the statement comes from the pope with his special authority from Christ and his access to the best advice, there must be solid reasons for doubting the papal judgement. The objector must therefore scrutinize his own claims to competence and also look for the effects of wishful thinking. Thirdly, any action which he takes must be for the good of the Church and not merely for his own satisfaction. 'Public protest should be used only as a last resort, because it easily does more harm than good.'[73] He should refer the matter to his parish priest, to the bishop and, if appropriate, to any of the structures being developed for discussion by a Church which increasingly values the insights of all its members. If the problem is still unresolved, all possible solutions having been seriously tried, the objector must follow the dictates of conscience, but making his intention no more public than is necessary. 'We should never leave the Church,' Father Yarnold concludes. If the conscientious decision should bring suffering or even persecution, 'we should reflect . . . that this kind of suffering has very often been the price that had to be paid for development of institutions among men'.[74]

Dissent within the Catholic Church is now a permanent feature of the Church's life. There is a limited analogy with the British parliamentary system where Her Majesty's Opposition is a respected part. The existence of dissent within the Church is only valuable in so far as it witnesses to the greater unity to which it belongs. Her Majesty's Opposition is above all loyal. It is not an enemy of the state. The critics within the Catholic Church are to be distinguished from the critics outside it. 'Dissent', declares Fr Avery Dulles, 'is a matter internal to the society in which the opposite position is normative. Dissent in the Church cannot be absolute. It occurs within the context of a larger agreement – namely, the acceptance of Christ as the supreme revelation of God and of the Church as the place where Christ is specially present and accessible.'[75] Father Dulles shows how the Council, while not explicitly allowing for dissent in the Church, in fact did so by adopting hitherto dissenting attitudes on biblical criticism, religious freedom, and secular systems of thought.

The toleration of dissent in the Church is bound up with the phenomenon called 'pluralism'. Defined philosophically as 'a system of thought which recognizes more than one ultimate principle',[76] the word has taken on wider meanings sociologically and theologically. In terms of culture, advances in the speed and ease of communications have meant that in most parts of the world a native culture exists side by side with other traditions of attitude and behaviour. But in theology, pluralism signifies the basic convictions which may be expressed in more than one way; or, if you like, that 'the Spirit's guidance may give rise to diverse forms of theology, law, custom, and piety within the Church',[77] and that fundamental concerns may operate through different and even opposing secondary convictions. Theological pluralism was discouraged in the Catholic Church after 1870, when a neo-Scholastic account of the faith became the one taught in all the seminaries. Theologians who tried to express the faith in terms shared with philosophers and scientists did so at their peril. Pope John's seminal phrase at the opening of the Second Vatican Council was the great charter legitimating pluralism: 'The substance of the ancient doctrine of the deposit of faith is one thing, and the way in which it is presented is another.'[78]

Pluralism and dissent are not to be identified, though there are many links between them. Pluralism allows for different ways of expressing the same truth. One way in which it operates is by allowing the faith to be expressed in the style most congenial to the faithful of a district. In worship, for example, Japanese Christianity could look different from Indian, and Congolese from Danish. The permissible limits will be determined by the need to safeguard the greater unity; we need not all like a particular style of worship but we must be able to recognize it. In doctrine and theology, pluralism will mean expressing the faith in different conceptual and philosophical frames and here the border with dissent will not be clear. Pluralism in discipline means accepting variant codes of behaviour through which the common faith may still be lived as well as believed. Again, there will be disputed territory. It will not be comfortable but, unless the Catholic Church is to shrivel into a sect within the pluralist world, it is not to be escaped.

It is already possible to examine the experience of pluralism and dissent through the analyses of people themselves involved. What, for example, does it mean to be a professional New Testament scholar, convinced of the value of historical criticism for recovering the foundation events of the faith, and also a committed Roman Catholic? Many Protestants might feel that such a person could survive only by keeping his professional integrity and his religious loyalty well apart. Otherwise he would find himself unable to follow the evidence along some path indicated. How could he, for instance, assent to any of the canons on Peter and the papacy put out by Vatican I?

The American Fr Raymond E. Brown is just such a person. Reflecting upon his part in the dialogue between Lutherans and Catholics, he takes up those three statements from Vatican I.[79] Biblical exegetes would need to ask questions about the historicity of Matthew 16 itself, let alone the propriety of describing the episode in terms of primacy, jurisdiction, and other anachronisms. The theologian would want to ask how full, supreme, ordinary, and immediate jurisdiction over every church and every member left any freedom in the Church and any power to counter possible abuses in the papacy. In ecumenical dialogue concerning such matters, does the Catholic scholar simply repeat the statements of Vatican I, causing immediate deadlock? If he does not, how can he remain loyal to his Church's teaching?

Brown's answer is to take his departure from the 1964

Instruction of the Pontifical Biblical Commission, which officially teaches that the Gospels are not blow-by-blow accounts of what actually happened but are based on the memories and traditions as those were shaped in the life of the earliest Church. 'Such a modifying reassessment of the historicity of the Gospels casts light on how the statements of Vatican I bearing on the historical role of Peter may need to be reinterpreted by the introduction of distinctions that were not conceivable for a previous generation of Catholic scholars.'[80] But is it not cheating to take statements made a century ago and reinterpret them by totally new historical methods? Here Father Brown appeals to *Mysterium Ecclesiae* and its recognition of the extent to which the dogmatic formulations of any period are conditioned by the assumptions of their own day. Later generations must not ignore or deny such formulations: they retain their authority. But their meaning may be clarified.

In a footnote Brown calls attention to a possible difference between himself and a Protestant scholar. The view is sometimes advanced that when in Mark 8.27–33 Peter is rebuked as a Satan who thinks the thoughts of men, not God, Mark is implying that the Twelve had become the spokesmen for a false understanding of Christ. In fact Brown thinks that view untenable on exegetical grounds. But he would in any case have trouble with it on theological grounds. Vatican II confirmed traditional Catholic belief in the inerrancy of Scripture in matters which affect salvation. That inerrancy could not be reconciled with the view that Mark wished his readers to believe that the Twelve had preached a false understanding of Christ. 'Such a thesis', he adds,

> is quite different from the suggestion that Mark retained the tradition that the followers of Jesus, including the Twelve, understood Jesus inadequately during his ministry and had to be rebuked by him, so that it was only after the resurrection that the Twelve became the proclaimers of Christian faith.[81]

Between those two positions passes the limit of Father Brown's critical loyalty.

Yet Brown as a New Testament scholar is far from conservative. He notes that the key Petrine passage 'You are Peter and on this rock . . .' does not feature in the Marcan and Lucan accounts of the episode at Caesaraea Philippi. He notes also the similarities between this Matthaean addition and the language which St Paul used in Galatians 1.16 to describe his own experience of the risen Lord ('reveal', 'son', 'not flesh and blood'). This leads Father Brown to think that 'Matthew has added to the traditional confession by Peter at Caesaraea Philippi an echo of the appearance of the risen Jesus to Peter (1 Corinthians 15.5), consisting of Peter's confession of Jesus as Son of God and a church-founding response by the risen Jesus'.[82] He adds that such a view is permitted to a Catholic scholar thanks to the Pontifical Biblical Commission's affirmation that 'the truth of the story is not at all affected by the fact that the Evangelists relate the words and deeds of the Lord in a different order and express his sayings not literally but differently'.[83] Father Brown's critical views fall therefore into the category of legitimate diversity rather than into that of dissent.

It would appear to be otherwise with Dr Jack Dominian, at least as yet. Dr Dominian is a psychiatrist whose work especially in marriage guidance has led him to believe that the Church needs a radically new sexual ethic. He is among those who believe that *Humanae Vitae* represents a retreat from the promising teaching of Vatican II's Pastoral Constitution on the Church in the Modern World. We are concerned now less with the merits of his own suggestions[84] than with the account which he gives of himself as a practising and loyal Catholic whose convictions lead him at some points into dissent. He cites the passage from *Lumen Gentium* about religious submission of mind and will. He fully acknowledges the basic structure and claims of bishop and pope. 'If their authority to teach is denied,' he asserts, 'there is no point in pretending to be a Roman Catholic.'[85] He calls attention to the process by which the subject matter to be taught is actually formulated and distinguishes between 'the authority to teach and how the conclusions of what is taught are reached', but he is clear that when a declaration has been made, even if not *ex cathedra*, 'it is required that the teaching is treated with reverence and adhered to as the authentic teaching of the Church. . . .'[86]

Dr Dominian insists that he has always worked loyally from that position; it is not for him or for any other individual to abrogate the declared teaching of the Church. He adds his conviction of the good intention of the Holy Father and his advisers in producing *Humanae Vitae* and the *Declaration on Sexual Ethics*. But what happens when there is disagreement over the best means of promoting the agreed end, in this case that of 'preserving Christian love within sexuality'? For answer he turns to *Lumen Gentium* IV, the chapter on the Laity:

> An individual layman, by reason of the knowledge, competence, or outstanding ability which he may enjoy, is permitted and sometimes even obliged to express his opinion on things which concern the good of the Church. When such occasions arise, let this be done through the agencies set up by the Church for this purpose. Let it always be done in truth, in courage, and in prudence, with reverence and charity towards those who by reason of their sacred office represent the person of Christ.[87]

Dr Dominian's professional qualifications are beyond question. His views, he insists, 'are but one way of conceptualizing the topic. There are others which will have to be considered before a new synthesis emerges.'[88] His own convictions may at present be those of dissent. But he holds them as a loyal churchman who has skills to offer and whose experiences in his own expert field have led him to conclusions which he cannot in conscience deny. He has thus followed the guidelines suggested by Father Yarnold. His views gain pastoral urgency from his claim that they articulate those of the 'new Church' which he sees emerging as a generation comes to maturity who never knew the Church and its attitudes before Vatican II.[89]

In that Dr Dominian makes common cause with Peter Hebblethwaite, whose figure of the Fourth Man epitomizes the new Catholic critical loyalty. The First Man was, according to a French analysis of 1966, the progressive supporter of Vatican II; the Second, his conservative opponent. The Third Man was the one who said A plague on both your houses and who retired to cultivate his garden. Ten years later, says Mr Hebblethwaite, the three have been joined by a Fourth. This Fourth Man remains within the Church, for he sees it as 'humanity in so far as it has recognized, however falteringly, its vocation in Christ'. Such people 'can no more leave the Church than they can take leave of humanity. To do so would be a form of spiritual suicide.'[90] Yet the Fourth Man never feels at home in the Church and he remains its continual critic.

Mr Hebblethwaite's Fourth Man, like Dr Dominian's emerging new Church, rates authenticity high among the virtues. He is an activist, a pragmatist, one for whom authority must vindicate itself in personal relationships. 'Love in personal relationships and social justice dominate the minds of the emerging Church as apologetics, obeying rules and regulations, authoritarian principles, and the salvation of one's soul dominated the minds of a previous generation,' writes Dr Dominian.[91] Orthopraxis is as important as orthodoxy, declares Mr Hebblethwaite. The Church to be convincing must be a community where all teach and all learn. 'The mother who teaches her child to pray, the student grappling with the doubt of a friend – they too form part of the magisterium.'[92] The Fourth Man may well feel more at home in a small, informal community than in the institutional Church. But perhaps that is a pity. It is just possible that he might learn something from the First Man, or even the Second. By himself he seems in danger of becoming a prig.

Hebblethwaite himself regrets the isolation. Not only does the Fourth Man need the Church, but the Church needs the Fourth Man to be 'the agent or at least the catalyst of change'.[93] By his demand for authenticity he will enable the Church to become in practice what it already is: the Body of Christ where the eye needs the hand and the hand the eye and both enjoy life-giving union with the head: the people of God on the move, not dug in. Emphasizing the Church's duty to 'continue to convey the essential Christian message and provide a credible context in which faith is possible', Hebblethwaite contrasts the disillusion of the Third Man, which led him out of the Church, with the Fourth Man's critical loyalty. 'It is unreasonable to demand a perfect faith, hope undimmed, inexhaustible charity. . . . The Church is the flawed embodiment of faith, hope, and charity.'[94]

The Church is on pilgrimage; it has not yet arrived. Mr Hebblethwaite wrote of the Third Man in *The Runaway Church*, a study of trends during the ten years after the Second Vatican Council ended in 1965. His two later books present a curious contrast. Towards the end of *The Year of the Three Popes* he gives reasons for hoping that John Paul II might become 'the spiritual leader, in freedom and love, of all Christians'.[95] But *The New Inquisition?* expresses his dismay that the Pope from behind the Iron Curtain, for all his post-Vatican II attitudes, is led by his 'Polish theology' to support the conservative and defensive Congregation for the Doctrine of Faith. Mr Hebblethwaite's passionate and immediate advocacy of Dr Schillebeeckx and Dr Küng in their very different encounters with the redoubtable Congregation make compulsive reading, but his comparison of the crisis of 1979–80 with that over the Modernists early this century may prove the most valuable part of the book. 'Theology is no longer an internal ecclesiastical affair for specialists,' he writes. 'It begins to involve the whole people of God. . . . In the Modernist crisis society was still in the paternalistic phase in which public opinion could be disregarded with impunity. But now ordinary people have been told so often in homilies that "*You* are the Church" that they have ended up by believing it.'[96]

The Catholic Church has had little experience of an educated laity. But loyalty is bound to grow more critical where an educated laity is encouraged to believe and act responsibly. The Fourth Man challenges the magisterium to treat him as a responsible adult, making constructive use of his expertise, his concerns, and his energies (and similarly, of course, of hers). The challenge to the Fourth Man and Woman is to remain loyal even where the magisterium feels obliged to reject constructively meant criticism. The situation is so new that for some time to come adjustments are sure to be painful.

5

Petrine primacy is above all a ministry. That means by definition it is a primacy of serving. Only as that is seen in practice will the papacy commend itself to those who now hold aloof. But today's stress on service is not simply expedient. In this matter expediency and truth walk hand in hand. 'Feed my sheep'; 'Strengthen your brethren'; 'You are Peter and on this rock I will build my Church.' Those are the commissions to service. It is in the service of his brethren that the Prince of the Apostles is most true to his own calling.

History shows that some elements of Christian truth were disclosed early, achieving close definition at a time when many others were little more than implications hardly realized. The primacy of Peter was one of them. We have seen that when in the nineteenth century it was at last dogmatically defined, the terms selected to describe it spoke directly to the needs of a Church threatened on all sides by forces that denied the autonomy of revealed religion. Even the Catholic states were anxious to control the Church. The First Vatican Council concentrated the defence of the Church in the person of the pope. The powers of death swirled around the Church built on Peter but they did not prevail. The defence succeeded but the cost to the defenders was great. Vatican I spoke all too well to the crisis of its own hour and the needs of a century later could only be met after the Second Vatican Council had developed its predecessor's teaching. We have examined aspects of the new style which the Church has adopted as it responds to the new demands of the day.

One service of especial importance in the modern world can be given only by the papacy: a centre of religious authority which is at once universal and personal. The Petrine ministry as it has developed in recent years is increasingly able to offer this service. The way in which the world is developing makes it more and more urgently needed. We may examine the need before considering the response.

Analyses of the way life is going are legion but certain elements recur: an accelerating thrust of change, technological advances which at once increase possibility and restrict choice, a move towards cultural uniformity in which minority traditions, though strenuously defended, face extinction. The world and its resources will be increasingly controlled and as better communications diminish the planet's effective size the present power blocs will either learn to live as neighbours in the global village or will fight until the victor exterminates its rivals. In either case, world government must come. Administrative problems will be less formidable with total computerization. The least tractable problems will be the human ones, satisfying the individual's inborn longing to be valued as a human being. The enemy will be the total control of a faceless benevolent bureaucracy, for the sectional tyrannies of today, horrific though they are, will cancel each other out within the next half-century. Depersonalization will threaten from two sides. The individual will be pressed to see his fulfilment in efficient contribution to the smooth running of the social machine, so that individual initiative and personal creativity will be potentially deviant. And authority will be so remote and so large that even those high in the implementation of policy will feel themselves to be the servants of some immutable force of history or destiny.

The culture which grows in such a unified technological world is likely to be utilitarian, conformist, and grey. Its ideology will be a closed humanism and, as in the past, people will seek relief from its sameness in a fantasy world, provided, if it is wise, by the omnicompetent state; or, if they are allowed, in drink, drugs, and sex. The determinism will encourage an updated astrology so that the horoscope will dominate any newspaper that survives. These things have already begun and with them is growing an almost intolerable longing for personal significance.

The truth which has been so greatly clarified over the last hundred years about the Petrine office in the Church can be seen therefore to match a widespread human need. The universal primacy of Peter gives his successor a direct pastoral relationship with each one of the faithful. The principle of collegiality ensures that this relationship does not usurp that of the local bishop, who is fully Christ's under-shepherd in his own section of the flock. Yet the flock is one and the individual Christian is directly the care of the 'man at the top'. The double relationship is acknowledged liturgically when prayer for the pope is coupled with prayer for the local bishop. Its effectiveness will depend upon how well the renewed stress on papal ministry as service is grasped at all levels of church life. The possibilities are enormous.

This ministry, at once personal and universal, could not be performed except by one who combines in his own person universal authority and responsibility for every individual. Eastern Orthodox Christians accept the authority of tradition, encountering it in the Liturgy as well as in the teaching guarded by the bishops. But the jealously protected independence of each autocephalous Church, with its profound involvement in national well-being, prevents any clear expression of that universal loyalty so much needed in today's unifying world. Much the same must be said of the Anglican communion of independent episcopal churches, though they enjoy neither a generally accepted doctrinal authority nor a unified tradition of worship. Where episcopal government is the highest authority, committee-style leadership must result; and however conscientious a committee may be, it does not readily provide a focus for personal loyalty. The theological notion of the episcopate, an authentic element in Catholic tradition, is too abstract. So are the several Protestant authorities of confessional loyalty. They are necessarily sectional rather than universal and their heavy emphasis on the intellectual prevents them from supplying the needs of all the faithful. The other, and supposedly more simple, Protestant appeal to the Bible and the Bible alone becomes in practice the following of what some accepted authority says the Bible says. Only in the Petrine ministry is there an authority which is at once a source of infallible revealed teaching, an historical institution, and a human being of flesh and blood. 'Stand up,' said Peter when Cornelius had fallen down at his feet to worship him. 'I too am a man.'[97]

The need for a personal centre to which all the Churches and their members may relate with immediacy is met uniquely in the Petrine ministry. The dry bones of that claim come to life in the four traditional 'notes' of the Church: one, holy, catholic, and apostolic.

The Church is one and that unity has many facets. It is God-given, the product of the divine will, created in Christ and through the Spirit. That means that it exists, a factor to be reckoned with here and now. But it is also an event, to be realized or denied in human relationships. It is the fellowship of the Spirit, as untrammelled as the wind, but it needs to be expressed within the boundaries of historical organization. It is wide enough to include all varieties of human culture and in binding together the generations it transcends time as well as space. Any definition of its presence will have to account for those and for many similar pairs of seeming contradictions. The one true Church already is and yet it demands concrete existence. Paradox is not to be avoided.

William Temple's famous dictum, 'I believe in the Holy Catholic Church and sincerely regret that it does not at present exist',[98] is therefore unacceptable (not that that great ecumenical pioneer would have meant it to be taken at face value). But equally unacceptable is a more sophisticated view which for many years I believed to be true: that the unity of the Holy Catholic Church exists now only in fragmentary, partly-grown form. The full realization of unity, on this view, belongs to the Last Day. Although in the sense of God's total purpose, where all moments must be simultaneous and successiveness is transcended, it does exist now, it must not be identified fully with any historically existing body, whatever claim that body may make. So the Roman Catholic claims are an example of that 'over-realized eschatology' which has appeared in many forms to distort Christian judgement since St Paul's tiresome first-generation Christians in Thessalonica.[99] Full Christian unity belongs to the 'coming great church';[100] and that had to wait upon divine intervention though patient ecumenical activity might encourage its progress.

The assessment of separated Christians which came out of Vatican II has made it possible for Protestants to examine Roman Catholic claims more positively; for no longer does a favourable estimate imply the virtual uselessness of the sacramental and other church life of Protestant as well as Orthodox Christians. For

> Some, even very many, of the most significant elements and endowments which together go to build up and give life to the Church itself, can exist outside the visible boundaries of the Catholic Church: the written Word of God; the life of grace; faith, hope, and charity, with the other interior gifts of the Holy Spirit, as well as visible elements. All of these, which come from Christ and lead back to him, belong by right to the one Church of Christ.
>
> The brethren divided from us also carry out many liturgical actions of the Christian religion. In ways that vary according to the condition of each Church or community, these liturgical actions

most certainly can truly engender a life of grace, and . . . can aptly give access to the communion of salvation.[101]

This more generous attitude has taken the bitterness out of the situation and has made possible the dialogue through mutual inquiry reflected in the argument of this book. But it has raised several fresh problems. If non-Roman church life has such high value, why is it necessary to insist on a return to Roman obedience as the goal of Christian unity? Would not a federation of independent bodies acknowledging with mutual respect their different paths of obedience to the common Lord be a better way? There are problems, too, of a more practical sort. The irritation aroused by Roman Catholic conditions for mixed marriage when the non-Catholic partner is a practising member of his or her own Church is increased in a time of ecumenism. Ecumenism indeed is a one-sided affair if the Catholics participating start from the assumption that they are alone fully the Church, other bodies being assessed on a scale of 'churchness' where full marks can only be awarded to those who accept the papal decrees. Relations may be more pleasant than in the days before Vatican II, but at least in those days you knew where you were.

The notion of ecumenical parity has in fact raised many hopes falsely. It is a notion that requires close examination. That Christians from Churches that have been separated for centuries should meet and talk is agreed. Dialogue should allow equal opportunity for all taking part to express their own convictions, which in turn should be listened to with the most serious concern for empathy. But we should not assume that with love and courtesy and careful listening and sweet reason, we shall find that differing beliefs have been reduced to a formula which all may endorse. We should be prepared, where all has been tried, to differ. We should not expect to deny what we believe to be essential parts of our belief for the sake of a quiet life, nor should we expect others to do so. An aspect of belief cannot be shed if it proves unacceptable.

One such aspect of Roman Catholic belief is that 'the unity of the one and only Church, which Christ bestowed upon his

Church from the beginning . . . subsists in the Catholic Church as something she can never lose. . . .'[102] Also, the positive assessment of 'separated Churches and communities as such'[103] is made despite the belief that 'our separated brethren, whether considered as individuals or as communities and Churches, are not so blessed with that unity which Jesus Christ wished to bestow on all those to whom he has given new birth into one body. . . . For it is through Christ's Catholic Church alone . . . that the fullness of the means of salvation can be obtained.'[104] Bernard Leeming, in commenting on the Decree of Ecumenism from which those quotations came, mentioned the fear of many Catholics lest ecumenism should lessen the urgency of Roman Catholic witness by playing down its distinctive claims. 'What do separated brethren lack?' he asks, echoing their question. He answers it from that passage of the Decree: 'That unity which Christ wished to bestow.'[105] It is the unity of full communion. Partial communion is indeed present; it cannot be avoided, for to be a Christian at all means to be related to Christ, and so to the Church, the single Church into which Christ gathers all his people. But without perfect ecclesiastical communion the connection is incomplete; there is dislocation.

And at the centre stands Peter. He is the sign of unity and to be in communion with the visible Church that claims to be built on him is to share fully in that unity which Jesus Christ wished to bestow.

> It was to the apostolic college alone, of which Peter is the head, that we believe that our Lord entrusted all the blessings of the New Covenant, in order to establish on earth the one Body of Christ into which all those should be fully incorporated who belong in any way to the people of God.[106]

To belong fully to the unity of the Church is to stand beside Peter.

The holiness of the Church also finds a focus in Peter. Sanctity in its individual members is of course no monopoly of the Roman Catholic Church. Indeed, the unmistakable sanctity of Christian lives to be seen in separated communities makes visible unity a practical quest. The Spirit of Christ speaks across the human divide, creating divine impatience over all that keeps brothers apart. Holiness consists above all in being set aside for God as Christ has made him known. Jesus was the holy man *par excellence* and Christian holiness is something of his quality rubbed off on other human beings. The holiness of Christians and the holiness of the Church thus marks off those people and that institution in ways similar to those which set Jesus apart from his fellow-men. Holiness therefore questions the human assumptions and values conventional at any given period, and may well reject them. In appropriate ways the holiness of Christ will mark both the Christian community and its individual members.

Christian holiness runs against the grain of the present time by insisting upon absolutes. It is able to go all the way with psychoanalytical or sociological understandings of behaviour without suggesting that wrong, once its causes are understood, is right. In Peter Berger's phrase, it 'relativizes the relativizers';[107] in Chesterton's, 'it is the only thing that frees a man from the degrading slavery of being a child of his age'.[108] Holiness is personally disturbing when it goes beyond what we want and shows us what we need; it leads not to complacency but to repentance and so crosses the threshold into new possibilities. The Church's holiness is marked by the divine image, and with the human only when that is remade in the divine. Those who refuse to be remade will reject it. St Peter is believed to have been crucified upside down.

Catholic means universal, for the whole, for all people, and for all things. The Catholic Church is therefore the Church for all. Its true contrast is not with Protestant but with either local or sectional. If the Church is one, then each local church is a particular expression of that one Church. A sect is by definition cut off, independent, exclusive, self-sufficient. All Christians who have shared in the biblical renewal of the last fifty years agree that the sectarian ideal is quite alien to the New Testament Church. All the main historic Christian denominations see their church life as a manifestation of the one Church. The ecumenical problem for all is the relationship between the denominations and the one Church. None of the old definitions seems to fit.

The Roman Catholic claim is that unity subsists in the Church in communion with the see of Peter, but that all Christian individuals and groups in their partial degree of communion belong there too. Its claim to catholicity draws strength from its extension throughout the world, an extension which is made from a single local centre. The combination of universal with local provides its particular strength.

Catholicity is not a matter of numbers, impressive though the size of Roman Catholic membership may be. The number which matters is the number of different human cultures represented. The Church which spreads out from Rome can appeal to all nations and people of every educational level can find a home there. Paradoxically, the sheer bad taste of much popular religion bears witness to its catholicity. Everyone can find there something which he cordially detests; but there can be few people who cannot find also something to delight, purify, and humble them.

The Catholic Church must be a bridge between earth and heaven. It is rooted firmly on earth, a human institution to which you belong, not an idea or an ideal to be embraced. Its catholicity extends over time as well as space, and in existing continuously through many periods of history the Church has taken forms suited to the passing moment. No doubt in the present time of increasing change the forms of Catholic life will change more quickly, yet its identity will persist.

In no other Christian body than the Roman Catholic Church can these features of continuity and change, of the universal and the local, be so clearly seen. Since the clarifications of the Second Vatican Council especially, it is poised to become even more fully in practice what it is by intention, the Church for all mankind. It is now possible to see how other, previously hostile forms of Christian obedience may find their truest setting within its single, universal framework.

Protestants have traditionally measured the fourth 'note' of the Church, apostolicity, by faithfulness to the apostles' teaching as found in the New Testament. Eastern Orthodox, Old Catholics and Anglo-Catholics stress continuity with the hierarchical structure that goes back to the apostles' time. Both claims have run into difficulty through the findings of historical criticism, and many people in both camps would now agree that from the first, the message was given within the life of the community, adapted to the changing needs of that community. Patterns of ministry also owed less to a divine blueprint than to the struggle for survival.

A climate of opinion where old slogans are questioned and revised opinions are possible makes it easier to understand from outside the particular Roman Catholic claims for their pope. The bane of the Protestant view is intellectual antiquarianism; that of the episcopalian, government by committee. The papal primacy suggests a third way, for it begins with the memory of Peter's primacy among the apostles; not that of a dictator, but that of one who received the gift of a particular revelation concerning Jesus and later another revelation concerning eligibility for Church membership: the two foundations of all church history. Peter traverses the earliest recorded Christian experience as fisherman and shepherd, the man of action, human in his strengths and weaknesses but followed with a protection that would not allow the work built upon him ultimately to fail.

It took centuries for the Petrine primacy to be widely recognized as the final institutional authority in the Catholic Church; though it is striking how naturally, almost casually, the few appeals that have survived from the first Christian millennium were made. The growth of the papacy is an integral part of European history and has naturally been assessed as such. Theological interpretation has as naturally taken the form of attacking or defending the particular forms of the institution. The climax of conflict came in 1870 with the dogma of papal infallibility. The issue was too clearly defined to leave room for manoeuvre. You accepted the claims or you rejected them.

Times have changed. Responsible Roman Catholics are as unhappy as Protestants with the package-deal approach which their predecessors often favoured. The Roman Catholic Church is as eager as its opponents to distinguish between essential truth and the accidents of its particular historical expression. Authority and hierarchy are no longer to be interpreted in wholly juridical terms and the Church's responsibility to the world is considered as well as its rights. All this encourages a new look at the meaning of apostolic, restoring to prominence the notion of being sent by God. 'I am Tradition,' Pope Pius IX is said to have replied to the criticism that the dogma of infallibility usurped the function of the Church's tradition. The reply today begins to seem less presumptuous than practical. It points to a third way alongside the Protestant appeal to the Scriptures and the Catholic appeal to episcopal consensus. The final human arbiter in matters of final importance is not a book or a committee but a person, his human fallibility protected from making disastrous errors by the power of God. With the trappings of curial power questioned from within as well as from outside, it is easier than it was to discern the features of the fisherman-apostle Peter, whom we might not have chosen to be shepherd, but whom Christ did.

6

My argument is complete. It remains to outline the consequences.

The renewal of the Roman Catholic Church at the springs of its own integrity has passed the point where the historic Protestant reproach of betraying the gospel message loses all force. In an earlier book I suggested that when that happened, two questions demanded a positive answer before the heirs of the Reformation followed the obvious course of seeking full communion with Rome. Have the claims which Rome makes for herself come to look inherently likely? And if so, can you see them being fulfilled in the Roman obedience as it is now developing?[109] To both questions I now return the answer Yes.

What then follows? The Petrine claims, once accepted, must be answered. Full communion with the see of Rome becomes urgent. The questions at issue concern the best way of effecting it.

The most obvious way is that of individual reconciliation with Rome, and no one who accepts the arguments of this book will easily face the prospect of indefinite exclusion from full communion. The Vatican II decree on ecumenism distinguishes between 'the work of preparing and reconciling those individuals who wish for full Catholic communion' and ecumenical action; 'there is no opposition between the two, since both proceed from the marvellous ways of God'.[110] There

x has it been prevented from making disastrous mistakes in the past?

may nevertheless be some uncertainty over which is the more appropriate. If a significant number of (say) Anglicans became convinced of the Roman claims, then corporate reunion, that long, forlorn hope of a few, is a serious possibility. Precipitate action by individuals 'turning Catholic' might prejudice the larger movement by drawing off and discrediting the very people who could influence Anglican opinion further towards reunion. Delicate issues of conscience are involved.

It is not within the scope of this book to suggest a practical plan for such reunion, but to urge the need for it. In that, there is nothing new. Writing in the symposium *A Pope for All Christians?*, Professor J. Robert Wright showed that almost from the moment of division, some Anglicans have been prepared to grant the pope a measure of primacy.[111] His section on 'What sort of papacy would *not* be acceptable to Anglicans?'[112] is weakened by its negative approach to Roman claims about in-fallibility and jurisdiction. It is unreasonable to expect the Catholic authorities to retract their defined teaching. As I suggested when discussing those matters earlier, the way ahead is to accept the definitions and advance from them by clarifying their meaning further. The Chadwick-Yarnold suggestions about patriarchal jurisdiction suggest one such line to be followed.[113]

And, forming a continuous accompaniment to such pioneering work, there is the teaching of the non-theological faithful. Not only must remaining stumbling-blocks be removed, but historical memories must be faced, their hatreds acknowledged and purged in the fire of shared Christian brotherhood. That is the agenda in depth.

Meanwhile the work of fostering mutual understanding must continue. The Anglican–Roman Catholic International Com-mission and similar bodies have an important task in per-suading their own church authorities to take their hard-won agreement seriously. Outstanding issues must be tackled and there is need for occasional gestures of goodwill. Massive Anglican irritation could be dispersed by a favourable reassess-ment of their orders of ministry, for instance, and by the rationalization of policy over mixed marriages. Roman Catholics would be reassured by evidence that Anglicans can speak with a single voice, and that they possess an authority whose decisions are generally respected. Do they intend seriously seeking full communion with Rome?

Both sides need to develop a new philosophy of church history, and to respect each other's interpretation of the past. It is not possible simply to return to the position of Thomas More and act as if the Roman supremacy had never been denied. Neither Church is the same as it was then. Acceptance of each other's corporate Christian integrity must carry with it a mutual absolution for the past. The Reformers acted in good faith in preferring the truth as they saw it to the unity of the Church, and so did the Catholics in the action which they took. Hindsight may suggest that on both sides the lights were dim, but both sides acted in accordance with those lights. The polarization which followed as Catholic and Protestant took up their hostile positions for the long haul through divided Christendom did not result in frozen wastes, for holiness and true religion found a home in both camps, as well as much that was superficial, bigoted, and downright wicked. An encouraging sign today is the zest with which Protestant and Catholic congregations sing each other's hymns.

If Anglicans now find the ground of their historic protest cut from under them, it is not a sign of their failure. If indeed Anglicanism is, as I hope, to lose its independence within the Catholic unity, it will be because its vocation is fulfilled. Rome has at last listened and learned. That which was held in trust for the whole Church within the Anglican boundaries has had its effect. Anglican return to Rome would signify not failure but success. In this connection, the influence of John Henry Newman may be especially important.

Should the Anglican Church continue an independent force, sustained by the momentum of its own past but with nothing distinctive still to stand for, that will be the failure. It will have missed the glad moment of its own *Nunc dimittis*.

Notes

PREFACE

1 J. Robert Nelson, in Peter J. McCord, ed., *A Pope for All Christians?* (SPCK 1976), pp. 177–93.

2 Longmans 1902.

3 Herbert Keldany in *The Times*, 28 June 1980. Maurice Villain, *L'Abbé Paul Couturier,* Casterman 1957, gives a charming picture of Spencer Jones in old age, p. 124, n. 35.

4 Faith Press 1959. I am grateful to Canon Roger Greenacre for lending me this book, as well as for reminding me of the importance of Spencer Jones.

5 SPCK 1944.

6 Weidenfeld and Nicolson 1969.

7 Doubleday 1980.

8 The papers at this conference were published as *L'Infaillibilité de l'Eglise*, Chèvetogne 1963 and included my report written for *Faith and Unity*, vol.6, no.6 (1962).

Chapter 1
APPROACH

1 *The Documents of Vatican II*, Walter M. Abbott, ed. (Geoffrey Chapman 1967), p. 715. (This book will hereafter be cited as *Docs. Vat. II.*)

2 *An Agreed Statement on Eucharistic Doctrine*, SPCK 1972.

3 *Ministry and Ordination*, SPCK 1973.

4 *Authority in the Church*, CTS/SPCK 1976.

5 SPCK 1976.

6 SPCK 1978.

7 *Crises Facing the Church* (Darton, Longman & Todd 1975), p. 81.

8 Ibid., p. 81.

9 Text published in *Church Relations in England*, SPCK 1950.

Chapter 2
DISCOVERING PETER

1 John 1.44.

2 John 1.40.

3 John 1.42.

4 Mark 1.17; Matt. 4.19; Luke 5.10.

5 Mark 3.16.

6 Matt. 10.2.

7 Mark 1.14.

8 John 1.44.

9 Mark 1.21, 29.

10 Acts 15.14; 2 Peter 1.1.

11 Matt. 26.73.

12 Acts 4.13.

13 Acts 3.1.

14 Mark 1.16; Matt. 16.17; John 21.15.

15 Mark 1.30.

16 1 Cor. 9.4.

17 Matt. 9.18–26.

18 Matt. 17.1–7.

19 Matt. 26.36–41.

20 Matt. 14.28–33.

21 John 6.66–9.

22 Mark 8.33.

23 Luke 22.31–4.

24 John 13.8.

25 John 13.36–8.

26 John 18.10.

27 Mark 14.50.

28 Luke 22.62.

29 1 Cor. 15.3.

30 John 21. 15–19.

31 Acts 2.14; 4.13; 5.3,8; 8.14; 9.32.

32 Acts 10.15.

33 Acts 11.18.

34 Gal. 2.12.

35 Gal. 1.18; 2.9.

36 Acts 11.18, 22–6; 13.2.

37 Matt. 16.13–23; Mark 8.27–33; Luke 9.18–22.

38 1 Cor. 1.12.

39 Gal. 2.12.

40 Acts 18.25; 19.7.

41 Acts 8.1; 3.13,20. See J. A. T. Robinson, *Twelve New Testament Studies* (SCM Press 1962), pp. 139–53.

42 John 20.8.

43 John 1.41.

44 John 1.49.

45 John 13.23; 18.15; 19.26–7; 20.2,4,8.

46 R. E. Brown, ed., Geoffrey Chapman 1974.

47 P. 39.

48 Matt. 17.1–8; Mark 9.2–8; Luke 9.28–36.

49 Acts 5.1–11.

50 Acts 10.9–16.

51 Acts 12.6–11.

52 2 Peter 3.15–16.

53 *Peter in the New Testament*, p. 166.

54 Ibid., p. 168.

55 See my 'The Human Integrity of St John's Jesus', in E. A. Livingstone, ed., *Studia Biblica 1978*, Sheffield 1980, vol. 2, pp. 75–8.

56 Mark 8.27–30. Compare Matt. 16.13–20; Luke 9.18.

57 Matt. 16.17–19.

58 See Oscar Cullmann, *The Early Church* (SCM Press 1956), pp. 39–58.

59 Matt. 16.21–3.

60 J. C. Fenton, *Saint Matthew* (Penguin Books 1963), p. 270.

61 Acts 5.1–11.

62 1 Cor. 5.3–5.

63 1 Cor. 12.3.

64 Acts 10.2.

65 Luke 22.31–4.

66 Luke 22.28–30.

67 Gal. 2.7–9.

68 1 Cor. 15.3–8.

Chapter 3
DISCOVERING THE PAPACY

1   Longmans, Green & Co., 7th edn, 1900.

2   *Bishop Gore and Roman Catholic Claims*, 1905.

3   Abridged and ed. H. F. Woodhouse. John Murray 1952.

4   *The Church and Infallibility*, Sheed & Ward 1954.

5   K. M. Ross, *Why I am not a Roman Catholic*, Mowbray 1953.

6   Oscar Hardman, *But I am a Catholic!*, SPCK 1958.

7   *Infallible Fallacies*, SPCK 1954.

8   *The Nightmare of Infallible Fallacies*, CTS 1955.

9   Longmans, Green & Co. 1956.

10 Longmans, Green & Co. 1958.

11 *Chrétiens Désunis*, Editions du Cerf 1937.

12 *Du Protestantisme à l'Eglise*, Editions du Cerf 1955; Eng. trans., *The Spirit and Forms of Protestantism*, Collins 1963.

13 *Introduction à l'Oecuménisme*, Casterman 1961.

14 SPCK 1952.

15 Darton, Longman & Todd 1962.

16 *No Apology*, p. ix.

17 *Peter: Disciple – Apostle – Martyr*, Eng. trans: (SCM Press 1953), p. 152.

18 Ibid., p. 231.

19 Ibid., pp. 237–8.

20 'The Tradition', in *The Early Church*, pp. 57–99.

21 Clement of Rome, 1 Cor. 42, Eng. trans., Maxwell Staniforth in *Early Christian Writings* (Penguin Books 1968), p. 45.

22 Matt. 28.17–20.

23 Clement of Rome, loc. cit., p. 23.

24 E.g. Dionysius of Corinth (*c.* A.D. 171), in Eusebius, *Ecclesiastical History* (hereafter cited as *HE*), 4.23 (Eng. trans., H. J. Lawlor and J. E. L. Oulton (SPCK 1954), vol. 1, pp. 128–30; Hegesippus, in Eusebius, loc. cit., vol. 1, p. 127; Irenaeus, *Adv. Haereses*, 3.3.2 (Eng. trans., F. R. M. Hitchcock, *Against the Heresies* (SPCK 1916), vol. 1, p. 85. These and other texts are conveniently assembled in E. Giles, op. cit., pp. 1–10.

25 1 Clem. 59, loc. cit., p. 54.

26 Clarendon Press 1959, p. 4.

27 Ibid., p. 5.

28 Ibid.

29 Eusebius, *HE*, 2. 23, Lawlor and Oulton, vol. 1, pp. 56–9.

30 Eusebius, *HE*, 3. 11, Lawlor and Oulton, vol. 1, p. 78.

31 Eusebius, *HE*, 3. 5. 3–4, Lawlor and Oulton, vol. 1, pp. 68–9.

32 Eusebius, *HE*, 3. 32. 1–4, Lawlor and Oulton, vol. 1, pp. 92–3.

33 Eusebius, *HE*, 3. 35, Lawlor and Oulton, vol. 1, p. 95.

34 Eusebius, *HE*, 4. 5. 1–6, 4, Lawlor and Oulton, vol. 1, pp. 106–8.

35 Eusebius, *HE*, 3. 32. 5–6, Lawlor and Oulton, vol. 1, p. 93.

36 Op. cit., p. 9.

37 Eusebius, *HE*, 5. 23–4, Lawlor and Oulton, vol. 1, pp. 168–70.

38 Op. cit., p. 10.

39 Ibid.

40 Ibid., p. 13.

41 Ibid., p. 14.

42 Ibid., p. 17.

43 G. Schwaiger in K. Rahner, ed., *Encyclopaedia of Theology* (Burns & Oates 1975), p. 1245.

44 G. Lyall, *Supernature* (Hodder & Stoughton 1973), p. 16.

45 Loc. cit.

46 Bede, *A History of the English Church and People*, Eng. trans. L. Sherley Price (Penguin Books 1955), p. 66.

47 Ibid., p. 89.

48 Penguin Books 1971.

49 P. 47.

50 Pallenberg, op. cit., p. 81.

51 *The Runaway Church* (Collins 1978), p. 82.

52 Ibid., p. 80.

53 The doctrine will be considered at length later; see especially pp. 105–10 and 128–30. For the present it should be remembered that (1) infallibility is not positive inspiration but negative protection from error; (2) it is a special case of what is claimed for the whole Church; (3) in *Pastor Aeternus* it is one aspect of the papal primacy which is there defined.

54 Vatican I did not, of course, ignore bishops; it is a matter of emphasis.

55 See J. Meyendorff, in P. J. McCord, ed., *A Pope for All Christians?* (SPCK 1977), pp. 129–47.

56 52 Ladbroke Grove, London W11 2PB.

57 *The Primacy of Peter*, Eng. trans., Faith Press 1963.

58 *Truth and Authority*, CTS/SPCK 1977. See also pp. 131–2.

Chapter 4
IMPLICATIONS

1   *No Apology*, p. ix.

2   1 Cor. 12.26.

3   In E. L. Mascall and H. S. Box, eds., *The Blessed Virgin Mary* (Darton, Longman & Todd 1963), p. 108.

4   For variant sources of this saying, see *Oxford Dictionary of Quotations* (Oxford University Press 1959), pp. 195.1 and 526.17.

5   Eng. trans. (CTS 1968), p. 10.

6   Ibid.

7   See above, pp. 46–7.

8   Burns & Oates, 18th impression (1947), p. vi.

9   Op. cit., p. 76.

10 Ibid., p. v.

11 Eng. trans., Mercier Press, 6th edn, 1963.

12 Pp. 9–10.

13 Quotations from this document are taken from the translation in Austin Flannery, O.P., ed., *Vatican Council II* (hereafter cited as 'Flannery'), Costello Publishing Company 1975.

14 *De Ecclesia*, 4.31, Flannery, p. 388.

15 Ibid., 4.37, Flannery, p. 395.

16 Ibid.

17 E.g. P. Hebblethwaite, *The Runaway Church*, pp. 94–5.

18 120 West Heath Road, London NW3 7TY.

19 *The Origin of Christology*, Cambridge University Press 1977.

20 Ibid., p. 2.

21 A convenient edition of Jewel's book is J. E. Booty, ed., *An Apology for the Church of England by John Jewel*, Cornell University Press 1963.

22 E.g. Bramhall, Cosin, Laud. See J. Robert Wright, in P. J. McCord, ed., *A Pope for All Christians?*, p. 181.

23 Eng. trans., SCM Press, 10 vols. 1964–77.

24 See James Barr, *The Semantics of Biblical Language*, Oxford University Press 1961.

25 K. L. Schmidt, *The Church*, A. & C. Black 1950.

26 K. H. Rengstorff, *Apostleship*, A. & C. Black 1950.

27   N. Geldenhuys, *Supreme Authority* (Marshall, Morgan & Scott 1953), p. 120.

28   *The Quest of the Historical Jesus*, A. & C. Black, pp. 370–1.

29   M. Werner, Eng. trans., *The Formation of Christian Dogma*, A. & C. Black 1957.

30   John Hick, ed., SCM Press 1977.

31   *The Myth of God Incarnate*, p. 139.

32   Ibid.

33   E.g. Origen, *Contra Celsum,* Eng. trans., H. Chadwick; Cambridge University Press 1953. Convenient selections in H. F. Stevenson, ed., *A. New Eusebius* (SPCK 1957), pp. 137–42.

34   E.g. Acts 5.1–11.

35   B. C. Butler, *Spirit and Institution in the New Testament* (Mowbray 1961), p. 18.

36   *When the Going was Good* (reprinted Penguin Books 1949), pp. 129–30.

37   SPCK.

38   *Doctrine in the Church of England*, SPCK 1938.

39   *Christian Believing*, p. 35.

40   Ibid., p. 36.

41   Ibid., pp. 37–8.

42   Ibid., p. 38.

43   Ibid., p. 39.

44   *The Resilient Church* (Gill & Macmillan 1977), pp. 29–45. Cf. below, pp. 26–88.

45   S. T. Coleridge, *Confessions of an Inquiring Spirit*, ed. H. J. Hart (A. & C. Black 1956), p. 42.

46   G. W. E. Russell, *Collections and Recollections*, ch. 6, in *Oxford Dictionary of Quotations* (Oxford University Press 1959), p. 335.

47   Eng. trans., Collins, Fontana 1963.

48   *The Spirit and Forms of Protestantism*, p. 172.

49   *The Resilient Church*, p. 191.

50   Ibid., pp. 191–4.

51   1 Cor. 1.26–8.

52   1 Cor. 2.8–10.

53   1 Cor. 2.10–11.

54   Matt. 16.15–17.

55   Rom. 1.19–20.

56   Acts 14.15–17.

57   Acts 17.23–7.

58   Acts 17.29–31.

59   Burns & Oates 1959.

60   Denzinger-Schönmetzer, *Enchiridion Symbolorum Definitionum et Declarationum*, Herder, 25th edn 1973 (hereafter cited as DS), s. 1501.

61   *The Spirit and Forms of Protestantism*, p. 166.

62   *De Revelatione* 9, Eng. trans., Flannery, p. 755.

63   Ibid.

64   Ibid., ch. 10.

65   Many of the more scholarly exponents of this view are associated with the UCCF (38 De Montford Street, Leicester LE1 7GP), formerly known as IVF.

66   See Raymond E. Brown, *Crises Facing the Church*, pp. 109–18.

67   Eng. trans., *What We Believe* (CTS 1973), p. 16.

68   Ibid.

69   On the coherence of Anglican theology, see Stephen W. Sykes, *The Integrity of Anglicanism*, Mowbray 1978.

70   *De Revelatione* 10, Flannery, pp. 755–6.

71   *De Ecclesia* 22, Flannery, p. 374.

72   *The Runaway Church*, p. 81; *The New Inquisition?* (Collins, Fontana 1980), p. 105.

73   1 Cor. 12.28.

74   Eph. 4.11.

75   Eph. 2.20.

76   Eph. 3.5.

77   *Encyclopaedia of Theology*, p. 871.

78   Ibid., p. 872.

79   Ibid.

80   Ibid.

81   Ibid., p. 873.

82   Ibid.

83   *The Catholic Church and Conversion*, Burns & Oates 1960 (first published 1926), p. 80.

84   Ibid., p. 81.

85   Matt. 18.15–20.

86   *What We Believe*, p. 9.

87   *The Fundamentals of Catholic Dogma*, p. 10.

88   Ibid., p. 297.

89   DS 3903, Eng. trans. in Paul F. Palmer, *Mary in the Documents of the Church* (Burns & Oates 1953), p. 113.

90   *De Ecclesia*, heading before ch. 68, Flannery, p. 422.

91   Eng. trans., *To Honour Mary*, CTS 1974.

92   Matt. 18.20.

93   John 1.14; 14.6; 1 John 5.20.

94   John 8.32; 14.17; 17.17; 2 John 1–3; compare Matt. 28.19f.

95   Rom. 1.16; 2 Cor. 6.7; 13.8; Gal. 1.17; 1 Thess. 2.2.

96   2 Cor. 11.14; Gal. 1.6; 2.5.

97   1 Tim. 3.15.

98   Matt. 10.40; Mark 9.37 = Matt. 18.5; Luke 9.48; John 13.20; 12.44.

99   E. L. Mascall, *The Recovery of Unity*, p. 250.

100   Gal. 1–2.

101   Avery Dulles, s.j. *The Resilient Church*, p. 121.

102   1943. Eng. trans., *The Mystical Body of Jesus Christ*, CTS.

103   Mascall, op. cit., p. 211.

104   *The Spirit of Catholicism*, Eng. trans., Sheed & Ward 1929.

105   *The Sheepfold and the Sheep*, Longmans, Green & Co., 1956.

106   *Infallible?* Eng. trans., (Collins 1972), p. 56.

107   Bishop Krementz quoted in Dulles, op. cit., p. 122 from Mansi, *Sacrorum Conciliorum Collectio*, vol. 52, col. 683B.

108   Dulles, loc. cit., citing *Collectio Lacensis* 7 (Freiburg 1890), pp. 350–1.

109   Dulles, loc. cit.

110   'The Primacy of Peter: Theology and Ideology', in *New Blackfriars* 50 (1969), pp. 347–55, 399–404.

111   Loc. cit., p. 123.

Chapter 5
RECOGNIZING PETER IN THE PAPACY

1   DS 3073, Eng. trans., H. Bettenson, ed., *Documents of the Christian Church* (Oxford University Press 1946), pp. 381–2.

2   1 Peter 5.1–4.

3   2 Cor. 11.29–30.

4   2 Cor. 12.9–11.

5   DS 3064, quoted from H. U. von Balthasar, *Elucidations*, Eng. trans. (SPCK 1975), p. 99.

6   Ibid.

7   *The Runaway Church*, p. 98.

8   *On Being a Christian*, Eng. trans. (Collins 1977), p. 498.

9   Matt. 16.16–18 followed by 16.22–3; Luke 22.32 followed by 22.34; John 21.15 followed by 21.20.

10 *On Being a Christian*, p. 500.

11 Ibid.

12 Ibid.

13 DS 3055.

14 DS 3058.

15 DS 3064.

16 *Elucidations*, p. 99.

17 Johann Nikolaus von Hontheim (1701–90), who wrote under the name Febronius, was the theorist of Gallicanism in the German states. For a favourable account of the Gallican and related opposition to papal primacy, see C. B. Moss, *The Old Catholic M.vement*, SPCK 1948.

18 In the next few paragraphs I am greatly indebted to Raymond E. Brown, *Crises Facing the Church*, pp. 109–18, which includes extracts from the most important documents.

19 *The Historical Truth of the Gospels*, Eng. trans. in J. A. Fitzmyer, *Theological Studies* 25 (1964), quoted in Brown, op. cit., p. 114.

20 Op. cit., p. 115.

21 *Docs. Vat. II*, p. 715.

22 Eng. trans., *What We Believe*, CTS 1973.

23 P. 14.

24 Ibid.

25 See above, pp. 110–14.

26 *De Ecclesia* 18; Flannery, p. 370.

27 Ibid.

28 Ibid., 20; Flannery, p. 372.

29 Ibid., 21; Flannery, p. 373.

30 Ibid., 22; Flannery, p. 375.

31 Ibid.

32 Ibid., 23; Flannery, p. 376.

33 Ibid., 25; Flannery, p. 375.

34 Ibid., 27; Flannery, p. 382.

35 *Infallible?*, p. 85.

36 Ibid., p. 87.

37 Collins 1976.

38 P. 500.

39 Above, pp. 15–19.

40 CTS/SPCK 1976.

41 CTS/SPCK 1977.

42 P. 30.

43 P. 31.

44 P. 34.

45 P. 35.

46 *Truth and Authority*, p. 34.

47 Eng. trans., *The Regulation of Birth*, CTS 1968.

48 See the accounts in A. M. G. Stephenson, *Anglicanism and the Lambeth Conferences* (SPCK 1978), pp. 121f., 149, 170–1.

49 Eng. trans., *Christian Marriage*, CTS 1965.

50 SPCK 1958.

51 *The Agonising Choice*, Eyre and Spottiswoode 1971.

52 Sections 47–52; Flannery pp. 549–57.

53 16, Eng. trans., p. 17.

54 *Contraception and Chastity* (CTS 1977), p. 18.

55 Ibid., p. 13.

56 Ibid., p. 14.

57 CTS 1970.

58 *Facing Up to Humanae Vitae*, p. 5.

59 Ibid., p. 12.

60 Para. 24.

61 Para. 17.

62 *The Runaway Church*, p. 216.

63 Para. 51; Flannery, p. 955.

64 Ed. A. Kosnik and others, Search Press 1977.

65 P. 46.

66 Eng. trans., CTS 1976.

67 Cf. Kosnik, pp. 50–2.

68 Horace, *Odes* 2. 10:

All who love safety make their prize

The golden mean and hate extremes. . . .

Eng. trans. (Penguin Books 1964), p. 108.

69   In *A Pope for All Christians?*, p. 5.

70   *De Ecclesia* 25; Flannery, p. 379.

71   *The Wit and Wisdom of Sidney Smith* (Longmans, Green & Co., 1860), p. 149; from a letter to Archdeacon Singleton.

72   *The Pope Speaks*, Living Parish Pamphlets 1968.

73   Ibid., p. 18.

74   Ibid., p. 19.

75   *The Resilient Church*, p. 47.

76   *Shorter Oxford Dictionary* (Oxford University Press 1959), p. 1528.

77   *Crises Facing the Church*, pp. 64–7.

78   *Docs. Vat. II*, p. 715.

79   *Crises Facing the Church*, pp. 64–7.

80   Ibid., pp. 65–6.

81   Ibid., p. 71.

82   Ibid., pp. 72–3.

83   Ibid.

84   *Proposals for a New Sexual Ethic*, Darton, Longman & Todd 1977.

85   Ibid., p. 13.

86   Ibid.

87   *De Ecclesia*, 37, *Docs. Vat. II*, p. 64.

88   *Proposals for a New Sexual Ethic*, p. 17.

89   Ibid., pp. 19–25.

90   *The Runaway Church*, p. 236.

91   *Proposals for a New Sexual Ethic*, p. 19.

92   *The Runaway Church*, p. 236.

93   Ibid., p. 238.

94   Ibid.

95   Collins, Fount 1978, p. 196.

96   Collins, Fount 1980, pp. 124–5.

97   Acts 10.26.

98   Quoted in F. A. Iremonger, *William Temple* (Oxford University Press 1948), p. 387.

99   1 Thess. 2.2.

100   The title of an important book by Theodore O. Wedel, SCM Press 1947.

101   *De Ecumenismo* 3; Flannery, pp. 455–6.

102   Ibid., 4; Flannery, p. 457.

103   Ibid., 3; Flannery, p. 456.

104   Ibid.

105   Bernard Leeming, s.j., *The Vatican Council and Christian Unity* (Darton, Longman & Todd 1966), p. 110.

106   *De Ecumenismo* 3; Flannery, p. 456.

107   *A Rumour of Angels* (Penguin Books 1971), p. 43.

108   *The Catholic Church and Conversion*, p. 78.

109   *Christ and the Human Prospect* (SPCK 1978), p. 89.

110   *De Ecumenismo* 4; Flannery, p. 457.

111   *A Pope for all Christians?*, pp. 176–93.

112   Pp. 194–7.

113   See above, pp. 58, 131–2.

Index of Names and Subjects

Index of Scripture References